CHILDREN'S ISSUES, LAWS AND PROGRAMS

WHEN ABUSE AND NEGLECT OCCUR AT RESIDENTIAL TREATMENT FACILITIES

CHILDREN'S ISSUES, LAWS AND PROGRAMS

Additional books in this series can be found on Nova's website at:

https://www.novapublishers.com/catalog/index.php?cPath=23_29&seriesp=Children%27s+Issues%2C+Laws+and+Programs

Additional E-books in this series can be found on Nova's website at:

https://www.novapublishers.com/catalog/index.php?cPath=23_29&seriespe=Children%27s+Issues%2C+Laws+and+Programs

CHILDREN'S ISSUES, LAWS AND PROGRAMS

WHEN ABUSE AND NEGLECT OCCUR AT RESIDENTIAL TREATMENT FACILITIES

KIRSTEN S. MADSEN
EDITOR

Nova Science Publishers, Inc.
New York

For permission to use material from this book please contact us:
Telephone 631-231-7269; Fax 631-231-8175
Web Site: http://www.novapublishers.com

LIBRARY OF CONGRESS CATALOGING-IN-PUBLICATION DATA

When abuse and neglect occur at residential treatment facilities / editor,
Kirsten S. Madsen.
p. cm.
Includes index.
ISBN 978-1-60876-965-0 (hardcover)
1. Youth--Abuse of--United States. 2. Rehabilitation centers--United
States. I. Madsen, Kirsten S.
HV6250.4.Y68W46 2010
362.73'20973--dc22-2010012260

Published by Nova Science Publishers, Inc. ✦ New York

CONTENTS

PREFACE

Residential treatment programs provide a range of services, including drug and alcohol treatment, confidence building, military-style discipline, and psychological counseling for troubled boys and girls with a variety of addiction, behavioral, and emotional problems. In October 2007, the Government Accountability Office (GAO) testified before the Committee regarding allegations of abuse and death in private residential programs across the country such as wilderness therapy programs, boot camps, and boarding schools. The GAO found thousands of allegations of abuse, some of which involved death, at residential treatment programs across the country and in American-owned and American-operated facilities abroad. This book examines the abuse and neglect that occur at some of these facilities and presents investigative reports and written testimony from relatives of victimized teens who have been affected by these programs.

Chapter 1 - Nationwide, federal funding to states supported more than 200,000 youth in facilities seeking help for behavioral or emotional challenges in 2004. Recent federal reviews and investigations highlighted maltreatment in some facilities, resulting in hospitalizations and deaths. This testimony discusses (1) what is known about incidents that adversely affect youth wellbeing in residential facilities, (2) the extent that state oversight ensures youth well-being in these facilities, and (3) the factors that affect the ability of federal agencies to hold states accountable for youth well-being in residential facilities. This testimony is based on GAO's ongoing work, which included national surveys to state agencies of child welfare, health and mental health, and juvenile justice for the year 2006. GAO achieved an 85 percent response rate for each of the three surveys. The work also included site visits to four states (California, Florida, Maryland, and Utah) and discussions with the Departments of Education (Education), Justice (DOJ), and Health and Human Services (HHS). Interim work related to this testimony was completed between November 2006 and March 2008, in accordance with generally accepted government auditing standards.

Chapter 2 - In October 2007, GAO testified before the Committee regarding allegations of abuse and death in private residential programs across the country such as wilderness therapy programs, boot camps, and boarding schools. GAO also examined selected closed cases where a youth died while enrolled in one of these private programs.

Many cite positive outcomes associated with specific types of residential programs. However, due to continuing concerns about the safety and well-being of youth enrolled in private programs, the Committee requested that GAO (1) identify and examine the facts and circumstances surrounding additional closed cases where a teenager died, was abused, or both, while enrolled in a private program; and (2) identify cases of deceptive marketing or questionable practices in the private residential program industry.

To develop case studies of death and abuse, GAO conducted numerous interviews and examined documents from eight closed cases from 1994 to 2006. GAO used covert testing along with other investigative techniques to identify, for selected cases, deceptive marketing or questionable practices. Specifically, posing as fictitious parents with fictitious troubled teenagers, GAO called 14 programs and related services. GAO did not attempt to evaluate the benefits of private residential programs and its results cannot be projected beyond the specific programs and services that GAO reviewed.

Chapter 3 - Residential treatment programs provide a range of services, including drug and alcohol treatment, confidence building, military-style discipline, and psychological counseling for troubled boys and girls with a variety of addiction, behavioral, and emotional problems. This testimony concerns programs across the country referring to themselves as wilderness therapy programs, boot camps, and academies, among other names.

Many cite positive outcomes associated with specific types of residential treatment. There are also allegations regarding the abuse and death of youth enrolled in residential treatment programs. Given concerns about these allegations, particularly in reference to private programs, the Committee asked GAO to (1) verify whether allegations of abuse and death at residential treatment programs are widespread and (2) examine the facts and circumstances surrounding selected closed cases where a teenager died while enrolled in a private program.

To achieve these objectives, GAO conducted numerous interviews and examined documents from closed cases dating as far back as 1990, including police reports, autopsy reports, and state agency oversight reviews and investigations. GAO did not attempt to evaluate the benefits of residential treatment programs or verify the facts regarding the thousands of allegations it reviewed.

Chapters 4, 5, 6 and 7 feature testimony before the U. S. House of Representatives.

Chapter 8 - Private residential treatment programs for young people offer a range of services, including drug and alcohol treatment, confidence building, military-style and psychological counseling for a variety of addiction, behavioral, and emotional problems. Many of these programs are intended to provide a less-restrictive alternative to incarceration or hospitalization, or an intervention for a troubled young person.

If you are a parent or guardian and think you have exhausted intervention alternatives for a troubled teen, you may be considering a private residential treatment program. These programs go by a variety of names, including "therapeutic boarding schools," "emotional growth academies," "teen boot camps," "behavior modification facilities," and "wilderness therapy programs."

No standard definitions exist for specific types of programs. The programs are not regulated by the federal government, and many are not subject to state licensing or monitoring as mental health or educational facilities, either. A 2007 Report to Congress by the Government Accountability Office (GAO) found cases involving serious abuse and neglect at some of these programs. Many programs advertise on the Internet and through other media, making claims about staff credentials, the level of treatment a participant will receive, program accreditation, education credit transfers, success rates, and endorsements by educational consultants.

The Federal Trade Commission (FTC), the nation's consumer protection agency, cautions that before you enroll a youngster in a private residential treatment program, check it out: ask questions; ask for proof or support for claims about staff credentials, program accreditation, and endorsements; do a site visit; and get all policies and promises in writing.

Chapters 9, 10, 11, 12, 13 and 14 feature testimony before the U. S. House of Representatives.

In: When Abuse and Neglect Occur at Residential…ISBN: 978-1-60876-965-0
Editor: Kirsten S. Madsen pp.1-19

Chapter 1

RESIDENTIAL FACILITIES: STATE AND FEDERAL OVERSIGHT GAPS MAY INCREASE RISK TO YOUTH WELL-BEING*

Kay E. Brown

WHY GAO DID THIS STUDY

Nationwide, federal funding to states supported more than 200,000 youth in facilities seeking help for behavioral or emotional challenges in 2004. Recent federal reviews and investigations highlighted maltreatment in some facilities, resulting in hospitalizations and deaths. This testimony discusses (1) what is known about incidents that adversely affect youth wellbeing in residential facilities, (2) the extent that state oversight ensures youth well-being in these facilities, and (3) the factors that affect the ability of federal agencies to hold states accountable for youth well-being in residential facilities. This testimony is based on GAO's ongoing work, which included national surveys to state agencies of child welfare, health and mental health, and juvenile justice for the year 2006. GAO achieved an 85 percent response rate for each of the three surveys. The work also included site visits to four states (California, Florida, Maryland, and Utah) and discussions with the

* This is an edited, reformatted and augmented version of a U. S. Government Accountability Office publication dated April 2008.

Departments of Education (Education), Justice (DOJ), and Health and Human Services (HHS). Interim work related to this testimony was completed between November 2006 and March 2008, in accordance with generally accepted government auditing standards.

WHAT GAO FOUND

Survey respondents from 49 states reported investigating complaints of youth maltreatment in residential facilities in 2006, including physical abuse, neglect, and sexual abuse, and 28 states reported deaths. There were no discernable patterns in the types of facilities involved, including whether facilities were operated by government or private entities, or located in urban or rural areas. State officials said that the number of maltreatment incidents was greater than the total reported to HHS—1,503 incidents in 2005--due to barriers in data collection and reporting, including inconsistent funding and authority.

States license and monitor residential facilities, but state agencies reported oversight gaps that may place youth in some facilities at higher risk for maltreatment and death. Some types of facilities are exempt from state licensing requirements—primarily state operated juvenile justice facilities and private residential schools and academies. Licensing standards did not always address suicide prevention and other common risks. State agencies reported an inability to conduct yearly on-site visits to facilities because of fluctuating levels of staff resources dedicated by states, and infrequently sharing negative findings from their oversight results.

HHS, DOJ, and Education hold states accountable for youth well-being, but federal efforts are hindered by the scope of the agencies' oversight authority and practices. Most notably, these agencies do not have the authority to hold states accountable for youth in private residential facilities unless they serve youth in state programs that receive federal funds. For facilities that were under federal purview, federal requirements did not always address the identified risks to youth—including such risks as suicide and inappropriate use of seclusion and restraint—and program requirements were inconsistent. In monitoring state compliance, federal agencies did not always include residential facilities in their oversight reviews.

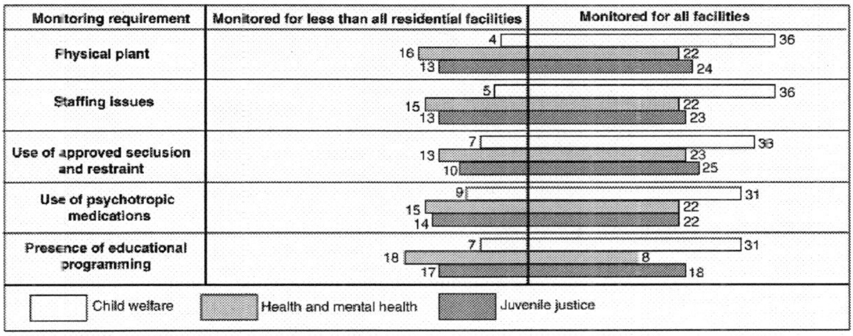

Source: GAO analysis of state agencies' responses to survey.

Note: Other agency responses included no such facility in state, don't know, and no response.

Aspects of Well-Being Monitored by State Agencies in Private Residential Facilities That Served Youth and Received Government Funding

Mr. Chairman and Members of the Committee:

Thank you for inviting me here today to discuss our ongoing work reviewing how state and federal agencies protect the well-being of youth in residential facilities who are receiving services for their behavioral or emotional challenges. Nationwide, federal funding to states supported more than 200,000 youth in government or private facilities in 2004. In addition, an unknown number of youth are placed in facilities by parents or others. These facilities include boarding schools and academies, boot camps, and wilderness camps. Overall, residential facilities play an important role in serving youth who cannot be safely served in their communities while living at home, due to risk of running away or harm to themselves or others. However, recent federal reviews highlighted youth fatalities in residential facilities due to neglect or maltreatment, and ongoing federal investigations continue to document incidents of abuse and neglect in some facilities for youth that in some cases have been severe enough to result in hospitalization or death.

As you know, states are primarily responsible for ensuring the well-being of youth in facilities and other settings, and do so by setting their own standards of care certain facilities must meet to obtain and maintain an operating license. Federal agencies also set requirements for youth wellbeing that states agree to uphold in exchange for receiving federal program funds, such as those administered by the Department of Health and Human Services (HHS) to support state systems of care for child welfare, mental health, and substance abuse; the Department of Justice (DOJ), for state juvenile justice systems; and the Department of Education (Education), for state education systems. Further, if patterns of maltreatment are identified and found to violate the civil rights of youth in certain facilities that are operated or substantially sponsored by state and local governments, the federal Civil Rights of Institutionalized Persons Act (CRIPA) authorizes the Attorney General of the United States to conduct investigations and bring actions against state and local governments. However, under the current regulatory framework, federal oversight authority does not extend to private facilities that serve only youth placed and funded by parents or other private entities. In some states, safeguarding youth in these facilities is the primary responsibility of parents and facility staff.

My remarks today will focus on the following issues with regard to youth well-being in residential facilities in terms of

1. what is known about the incidents that adversely affect the well-being of youth in residential facilities,
2. the extent that state oversight ensures the well-being of youth in residential facilities, and
3. the factors that affect the ability of federal agencies to hold states accountable for youth well-being in residential facilities.

This testimony was developed using multiple methodologies, and was limited to residential facilities we defined as those that require youth— ages 12 through 17—to reside at the facility and that provide program services[1] for youth with behavioral and emotional challenges. We surveyed three state agencies—child welfare, health and mental health, and juvenile justice[2]—about residential facilities that were government operated, privately operated that received government funds, and privately operated with no government funding. To further our understanding, we visited four states—California, Florida, Maryland, and Utah—and interviewed relevant officials. These states were selected based on the diversity of their state licensing and monitoring policies for residential programs, reports of child maltreatment, and geographic location. The scope of our work did not include the quality of services provided at residential facilities. We also obtained data from HHS's National Child Abuse and Neglect Data System (NCANDS); reviewed federal statutes, regulations, and guidance; and interviewed HHS, DOJ, and Education officials, as well as national association representatives and other experts on residential facilities for youth. The scope of our work did not include the quality of services provided at residential facilities. We performed our work between November 2006 and March 2008, in accordance with generally accepted government auditing standards.

IN SUMMARY

- Youth maltreatment and death occurred in government and private residential facilities across the nation, according to states we surveyed; however, data limitations hinder efforts to quantify the full extent of the problem. State-reported data collected by HHS in 2005 showed 1,503 incidents of maltreatment by facility staff in 34 states, including physical abuse, neglect or deprivation of necessities, and sexual abuse. Moreover, 28 states responding to our survey reported at least one death in residential facilities in 2006, with accidents and suicides among the most common types of fatalities. These reported data, however, did not capture information from all facilities. Many states lack authority under state law to collect data on exclusively private facilities, and data that states did report were often incomplete. As a result, the number of adverse incidents was likely more numerous and widespread than reported.
- All states have processes in place to license and monitor certain residential facilities, but states reported oversight gaps that may place youth in some facilities at higher risk for maltreatment and death. Most notably, state agencies exempted some types of government and private facilities from licensing requirements altogether, primarily juvenile justice facilities and private schools and academies. In addition, licensing standards do not always address suicide and other common risks to youth well-being. Although monitoring is key to ensuring facility compliance with standards, agencies in states we visited reported an inability to conduct yearly on-site reviews of conditions at each facility, because of fluctuating levels of staff resources committed by the state. Similarly, although information sharing can strengthen oversight for facilities shared by multiple agencies, many state agencies reported that they did not routinely share information with other state agencies about negative findings or when facility licenses were suspended or revoked.
- HHS, DOJ, and Education all have processes to hold states accountable for the well-being of youth, but federal efforts are

hindered by the scope of the agencies' oversight authority and monitoring practices. Most notably, these agencies do not have the authority to hold states accountable for youth well-being in private residential facilities unless they serve youth in state programs that receive federal funds. For facilities under federal purview, federal requirements did not always address the primary risks to youth well-being, such as suicide, and requirements were inconsistent among programs. In monitoring state compliance, federal agencies did not always include residential facilities in their oversight reviews.

YOUTH MALTREATMENT OCCURRED IN FACILITIES ACROSS THE NATION, BUT DATA ARE LIMITED AND NOT USED TO TARGET FEDERAL CIVIL RIGHTS INVESTIGATIONS

Nearly all states (49) responding to our survey reported investigating complaints of youth maltreatment in residential facilities in 2006, including facilities operated by government as well as private entities, and located in both urban or rural areas. The types of maltreatment reported by states included physical abuse, neglect or deprivation of necessities, and sexual abuse that sometimes resulted in hospitalization or death. State reported data to NCANDS from 2005 showed that 34 states reported 1,503 incidents of youth maltreatment by facility staff. Of these incidents, neglect or deprivation of necessities was the most frequent cause of youth maltreatment, followed by physical abuse, as shown in figure 1.

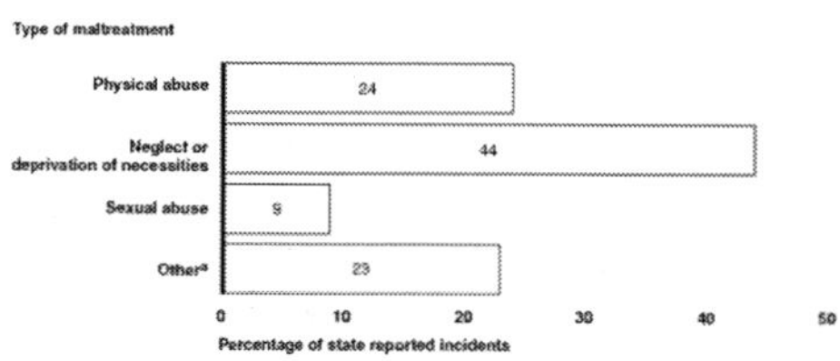

Source: NCANDS.

[a] "Other" incidents of youth maltreatment states reported to NCANDS include medical neglect and psychological or emotional maltreatment.

Figure 1. Percentage of State-Reported Incidents of Youth Maltreatment by Residential Facility Staff, Fiscal Year 2005

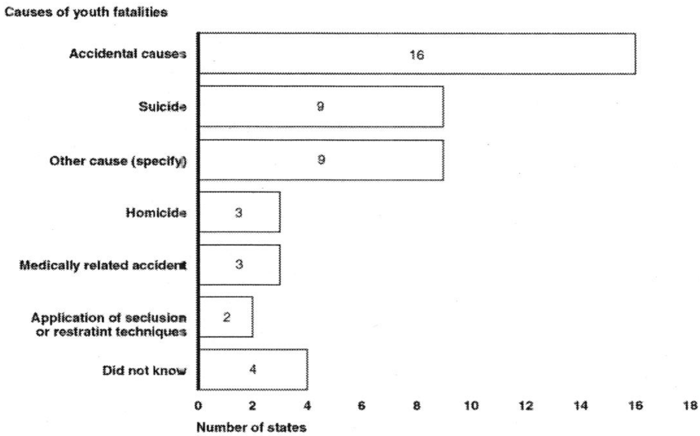

Source: GAO analysis of state agency responses to survey.

Notes: The survey question was as follows: Of the total youth deaths that you reported, how many died from each of the following causes: (a) suicide, (b) homicide, (c) application of seclusion and restraint techniques, (d) medically related accident, (e) accident that occurred while in a runaway or absence without leave status, (f) other accidental cause, and (g) other causes?

Other causes of youth fatalities in residential facilities include natural causes, choking, and internal bleeding.

Figure 2. Number of States That Reported Specific Causes of Youth Fatalities in Residential Facilities, 2006

Of the states we surveyed, 28 reported that at least one youth had died in a residential facility in 2006. These deaths were primarily due to accidents and suicide, but also due to homicide and application of seclusion and restraint (see figure 2).

Overall, officials from the states we visited said that the number of maltreatment incidents and deaths was greater than reported due to barriers in collecting and maintaining data. When available, comprehensive reporting of incident data can be used by state and federal agencies to assess the extent of maltreatment in residential facilities, inform risk assessments, target oversight resources, and develop policies to address trends. However, the lack of authority under state law hinders many states from collecting data on certain facilities—such as exclusively private facilities—and expanding oversight to cover them. In addition, states that have such authority reported difficulties sustaining data collection in times of budget shortages. National data in NCANDS for 2005—derived from state reports—suffers from these same limitations, as well as others. First, some states did not report data for residential facilities to NCANDS,[3] so the data may understate the number of maltreatments and fatalities. Second, many states (37) did not consistently identify whether the individual maltreating youth was facility staff, a parent, or other individual. Last, NCANDS only tracked fatalities resulting from maltreatment, not suicide or accidents that may be an indicator of neglect or other problem that needs resolution.

In the states we visited, youth maltreatment in facilities was attributed to several factors—such as a lack of experienced staff, insufficient staff training, or lack of appropriate supervision—particularly in smaller facilities. For example, county officials in one state told us that adverse incidents were most likely to occur in contractor operated six-bed group homes—frequently used by state probation and child welfare agencies— where the state reimbursement rate is generally not high enough to hire skilled personnel and provide staff with ongoing training, support, and oversight.

However, while in most facilities youth maltreatment may occur infrequently as a result of isolated circumstances, investigations of government and private facilities serving youth conducted under DOJ's Civil Rights Division (Division) have found a pattern or practice of civil rights violations in some facilities, including physical and sexual abuse, medical neglect, and inadequate education. At the end of fiscal year 2006, the latest year for which data were available, federal investigators reported active cases involving over 175 facilities in 34 states.[4] Annual reports from DOJ over the past several years have documented their findings of youth maltreatment in certain juvenile justice or mental health facilities:

Physical and sexual abuse occurred without management intervention. In one facility, staff hit youth and slammed them to the ground. Staff hog-tied and shackled youth to poles in public places, and girls were forced to eat their own vomit if they threw up while exercising in the hot sun. Staff routinely broke and wired shut the jaws of youth who showed disrespect in another facility. In some facilities, staff engaged in sexual acts with boys. Youth-on-youth violence occurred on an almost daily basis in some facilities, at times resulting in injuries that required hospitalization. Youth were sexually assaulted and threatened with sexual assault by other youth in some facilities, all without effective intervention from management.

Severe neglect resulted in poor education, suffering, and death. In a 1-year period at one facility, three boys committed suicide. In one suicide, staff lacked the appropriate tool to cut the noose from a victim's neck and also did not have oxygen in the tank they brought to help resuscitate him. The dental clinic at one facility was full of mouse droppings, dead roaches, and cobwebs; medications in the cabinet had expired over 10 years ago. In a state-operated mental health facility used by adolescents, older psychotropic medications, with serious side effects, were administered to sedate patients. One adolescent received 22 such psychotropic sedatives over a 2-month period. In another facility, youth were not provided with special education services as required by federal law.

The Special Litigation Section of DOJ's Civil Rights Division receives more credible allegations of violations of youth rights than it can investigate. During fiscal year 2005 alone, the Division received approximately 5,000 citizen letters; hundreds of telephone complaints, and 135 inquiries from Congress and the White House. Division officials stated that with additional sources of information, they could better target their scarce investigative resources. Officials said that receiving more detailed information from NCANDS on the incidents of maltreatment and death occurring in specific facilities would be helpful, as would the results of federal agency monitoring reviews of states that highlight findings related to residential facilities. Except in one instance,[5] officials said that no federal agencies—including HHS, Education, and DOJ's Office of Juvenile Justice and Delinquency Prevention (OJJDP)—were coordinating with the Division to provide pertinent oversight results.

Gaps in State Oversight of Residential Facilities May Place Well-being of Some Youth at Risk

All states have processes in place to license and monitor certain residential facilities, but our survey identified several gaps that allow some of the common causes of youth maltreatment and death to go unaddressed. These gaps include the fact that some types of government and private facilities are exempt from licensing requirements, licensing standards do not always address the primary causes of youth maltreatment and death, and state agencies inconsistently monitor and enforce facility compliance and share their monitoring results.

Certain Facilities Are Exempt from State Licensing Requirements

Licensing all facilities in a state—government or private facilities—can help ensure that residential facilities meet relevant state standards. Among state-operated facilities, however, more than half (28) of juvenile justice agencies reported exempting facilities from licensing.[6] In addition, many state agencies reported that certain types of private facilities were also exempt from licensing, regardless of whether they received some government funding or were exclusively private. Private residential schools and academies—a category that includes boarding schools and training or reform schools—were exempted more often from licensing than other types of private facilities, according to survey respondents. Conversely, treatment facilities were the type most commonly required to have a license. Agencies in six states reported they exempted faith-based facilities from licensure.[7] In addition, many agencies reported not knowing the licensing status of certain types of private facilities or reported that they did not have certain types of facilities in their state.[8] Some states are considering laws that would expand their licensing authority for private facilities.

One reason that private residential facilities may be exempt from licensing requirements is that state agencies do not have the necessary statutory or regulatory authority. Regarding residential schools and academies, for example, all agencies in 15 of the 33 states that responded to all three agency surveys reported that they did not have either the authority or the regulatory responsibility to license these facilities.[9]

The lack of licensing for all facilities serving youth has several consequences, in that there are no commonly accepted definitions of facility types. Within individual states, facility operators may bypass state licensing requirements by self-identifying their business as a type that is exempt from state licensing. In Texas, for example, a residential program self-identified as a private boarding school is not regulated by the state licensing agency, but the same facility would require a license if it self- identified as a residential treatment center or therapeutic camp. Inconsistent licensing practices across states can have implications as well. For example, a 2007 directory showed that Utah, which only recently implemented licensing requirements covering wilderness camps, was home to over 25 percent of registered wilderness programs in the United States.

Facility licensing is also important because parents and others considering placing youth in private facilities at their own expense do not always have the information they need to screen facilities and make an informed decision. In our testimony on private facilities last October,[10] we described cases in which program leaders told parents their programs could provide services that they were not qualified to offer, claimed to have credentials in therapy or medicine that they did not have, and led parents to trust them with youth who had serious mental disabilities. One national association for programs serving youth with behavioral and emotional difficulties testified before Congress that state licensing was important because the field does not currently have the capacity to certify facility integrity.

Some states are considering laws that would expand their licensing authority for private facilities, while some use other methods to provide protections for youth. For example, Florida, among other states, includes requirements addressing youth well-being in contracts facilities must sign to serve youth under state care. Florida officials estimated that 85 percent of residential facilities in the state's juvenile justice system are private facilities under contract with the state. The agency uses the contract provisions to help ensure that facilities provide youth with needed services in compliance with agency regulations as well as state statutes.

Accreditation is another method used by some states in lieu of, or to augment, state licensing requirements. For example, Ohio and Wyoming require specific health-related facilities to obtain accreditation instead of licensure as a condition to serving youth under state care. Of the states responding to our survey, a greater number of health and mental health agencies reported requiring facilities to be accredited by private organizations, due in part to conditions of participation for certain federal programs.[11] The accreditation process may require providers to meet higher standards than those required by state licensing bodies; however, accreditation does not necessarily ensure the safety and well-being of youth. Officials from an accrediting organization told us that they do not always inform the state if a facility's accreditation status has been suspended or limited. In general, fewer states reported requiring accreditation than not across the three agencies we surveyed.

State Licensing Standards Do Not Address Some Primary Risks to Youth Well-being

Our survey results showed that the licensing standards that states have in place for certain government and private residential facilities address many, but not all, of the most common risks to youth well-being that states had identified in our survey. The extent that state licensing standards cover the various aspects of youth well-being is important to safeguard youth from harm. Almost all states reported that when they required licensing, they required facilities to meet standards related to the safety of the physical plant, proper use of seclusion and restraint techniques, reporting of adverse incidents, and qualification requirements and background checks for staff.[12] These standards can help reduce the risk of harm due to accidental causes and staff maltreatment. However, other requirements addressing risks to youth are less often included as a part of licensing. For example, while states reported that almost all juvenile justice facilities are required to have written suicide prevention plans, about a third of state child welfare and health and mental health agencies reported that they do not have similar requirements for government facilities. In addition, most of the agencies in our survey did not require private facilities to have written suicide prevention plans.

State Practices Inconsistent in Monitoring and Enforcing Facility Compliance

State agencies reported monitoring youth well-being in residential facilities, but survey results showed that certain aspects of youth wellbeing were not included in all monitoring activities, as shown in figure 3. Periodic on-site reviews to monitor and enforce facility compliance help ensure that licensing standards are taken seriously and that risks to youth well-being are quickly addressed. Among six different aspects of youth well-being we asked about in our survey, the quality of educational programming and the use of psychotropic medications were most likely to be reviewed at only some or none of the facilities monitored by child welfare, health and mental health, and juvenile justice agencies. Conversely, staffing issues were most often included in all monitoring reviews of government and private facilities.

In addition, three of the four states we visited reported that they were unable to meet their goals for conducting annual monitoring visits at residential facilities due to a lack of resources. States reported that visiting facilities was necessary at least once a year, if not more often, to ensure that conditions for youth had not changed due to changes in personnel, ownership, or funding. However, the number of facilities visited each year depended on the fluctuating levels of resources committed by the state.

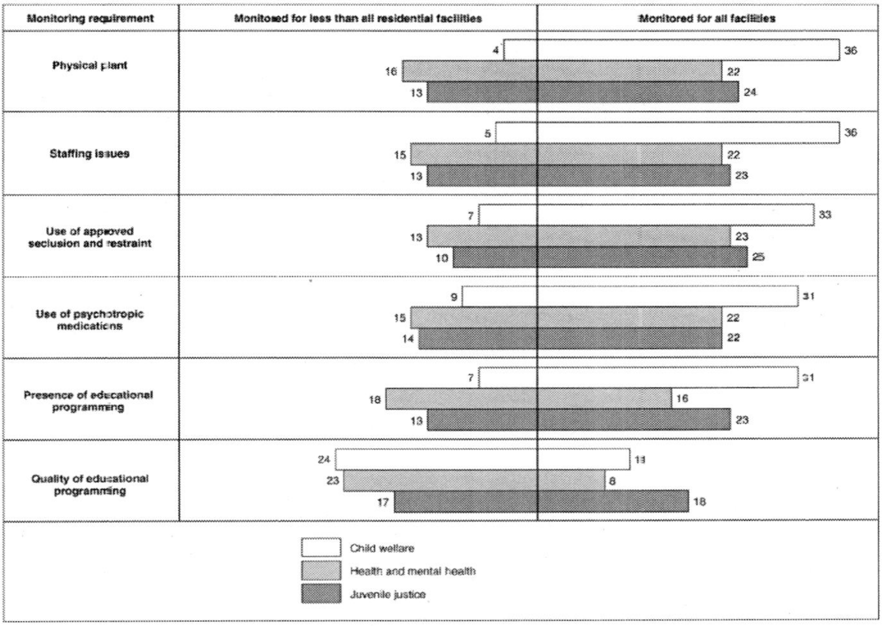

Source: GAO analysis of state agencies' responses to survey.

Note: The survey question was as follows: In 2006, did your agency routinely monitor or follow-up, or authorize for monitoring or follow-up, any of the following issues—in the absence of a complaint—at private residential facilities that received government funding providing targeted services for youth? Response options for this question were: (a) yes, monitored for all; (b) yes, monitored for some; (c) no, did not monitor; (d) no such facility in the state; (e) don't know; (f) no response.

Figure 3. Aspects of Well-Being Monitored by State Agencies in Private Residential Facilities That Served Youth and Received Government Funding

In Maryland, agency officials said that state resources were redirected, as necessary, to meet state goals for monitoring residential facilities for youth. In Florida and Utah, however, agency officials said that imbalances between the current workload and staff resources constrained the state's capacity to conduct efficient, effective, and timely monitoring of residential facilities. A facility operator in California said that on-site monitoring had been as infrequent as once every 5 years.

State agencies reported taking actions against facilities with identified problems in the last 3 years, but few reported suspending or revoking a facility's operating license. Options used included increased monitoring or requiring corrective action plans. Maryland state officials said that they may be less likely to close facilities when they fall below state standards if there is a shortage of facilities in the state and closing the facility would limit the state's ability to serve the youth who would be displaced by a closing. In addition, these officials noted that shutting down a facility is extremely disruptive to the youth who are placed there.

State Agencies Reported a Lack of Coordination to Share Oversight Results

Many state agencies reported that they did not routinely share information with others regarding negative findings from their monitoring reviews. State agency coordination to share monitoring results can strengthen oversight in situations where facilities are used by multiple agencies and can help ensure that youth are not placed in facilities that another agency has already identified as having problems. However, one or more state agencies reported that they did not routinely share reports of adverse incidents (17) or when facility licenses had been suspended or revoked (12).

Improving coordination among agencies across states is also important because almost all states reported in our survey that they placed some youth in out-of-state residential facilities. For example, child welfare agencies in the top 5 states reported placing over 3,500 youth in at least 26 states. Out-of-state placement can be difficult to manage, but may be used when the demand for services exceeds the state's capacity, particularly for cases requiring highly specialized services—such as therapeutic treatment for youth who committed arson, or who were involved in gangs. State agencies or parents may also place youth in other states where family members reside. Interstate coordination is important is to ensure that agencies sending youth for placement in other states are able to screen out facilities that have had negative findings uncovered during monitoring reviews or have outstanding allegations of maltreatment. Information sharing about adverse conditions in facilities may be particularly important in cases where state licenses cannot serve to help in making appropriate placement decisions. Four of the top five states that received the greatest number of out-of-state placements—according to child welfare agencies we surveyed—exempted one or more types of facilities from state licensing requirements.

FEDERAL AGENCIES CHALLENGED TO ADDRESS WEAKNESSES IN STATE OVERSIGHT OF RESIDENTIAL FACILITIES

HHS, DOJ, and Education hold states accountable for youth well-being in certain residential facilities, but their scope of authority is limited, and gaps in agency oversight practices result in inconsistent protections for youth. Most notably, these agencies can hold states accountable for conditions in facilities that serve youth through programs supported by federal funds[13]—whether government or private—but cannot hold states accountable for conditions in facilities that are exclusively private. When federal agencies do have oversight authority under certain federal programs, however, they do not always hold states accountable for addressing some of the primary risks to youth well-being. For example, in comparing requirements across HHS, DOJ, and Education, only HHS reported requiring states to address abuse and neglect prevention under certain federal programs. (See table 1.)

Federal program requirements are limited even for risks such as suicide, a problem documented by several federal agencies. For example, the Centers for Disease Control and Prevention (CDC)—which is part of HHS—have identified suicide as the third leading cause of death in 2004 among all U.S. youth,[14] and suicide was one of the leading causes of death among youth in residential facilities, as reported by states in this study. In addition, a study commissioned by DOJ recommends increased mental health screening for suicide prevention among incarcerated youth.[15] DOJ officials we spoke with generally agreed with the need to focus on suicide prevention in residential facilities, and suggested that additional federal requirements in this area would be helpful. DOJ and HHS have Web sites that list resources states can use for this purpose, but HHS officials said that states are more responsive to a requirement or more specific agency guidance.

Similarly, federal programs also do not generally require that states ensure the proper use of seclusion and restraint practices, which have come under intense scrutiny in recent years. Researchers and clinicians have chronicled the inherent physical and psychological risks in each use of these types of interventions—including death, disabling physical injuries, and significant trauma.

Table 1. Federal Program Requirements for States that Address Certain Risks to Youth Well-being in Residential Facilities

Agency and program area	Abuse and neglect prevention	Suicide prevention	Use of seclusion and restraint	Education quality
HHS				
Child welfare	Yes	No	No	Yes
Medicaid	Yes	Yes	Yes[a]	No
Substance abuse and mental health	Yes	No	No	No
DOJ				
Juvenile justice and delinquency prevention	No	No	No	No
Education				
Elementary and secondary education	No	No	No	Yes[b]
Special education and rehabilitative services	No	No	No	Yes[b]

Source: Analysis of HHS, DOJ, and Education documents.

[a]Applies only to psychiatric residential treatment facilities.

[b]Applies only to public agencies and children placed by public agencies in private facilities.

Currently, federal seclusion and restraint requirements cover youth placed in psychiatric residential treatment facilities that receive Medicaid payments. However, requirements do not extend to other types of facilities, and federal officials told us that these techniques continue to be used in ways that sometimes cause injury and death. HHS is preparing a draft notice of proposed rulemaking concerning the use of seclusion and restraint in non-medical community-based children's facilities.[16]

Federal agencies have several means of oversight for youth well-being, but perhaps one of the most rigorous is unannounced site visits to the youth's place of residence. According to the federal and state officials we spoke with, only an on-site visit to the facility can reveal whether services in the administrative reports are provided under conditions that ensure youth well-being. For example, DOJ officials observed that students in one of the facilities they visited received their educational instruction while in cages, and reported that it would have been difficult to detect this practice in an administrative review.

Among the federal agencies we reviewed, all included visits to states to ensure compliance with federal requirements, but agencies did not always include visits to residential facilities. DOJ officials target juvenile justice facilities, such as correctional facilities and detention centers, during on- site reviews, but HHS officials do not necessarily include residential facilities in their oversight reviews of state child welfare systems. HHS selects a sample of child case files for site visits, and because most children are in foster home settings, residential facilities are usually not included.

Similarly, while federal programs contain provisions agencies can use to enforce state compliance with federal requirements, these provisions vary in their rigor and use, and only DOJ has levied financial penalties.[17] To date, HHS and Education have required state corrective action plans as a method of enforcement, but officials said that they may also assess financial penalties in the future.

CONCLUDING REMARKS

As the results of our work show, protecting youth in residential facilities— many of whom are troubled and vulnerable to harm from themselves or from others—requires particular vigilance on the part of parents and responsible government agencies. However, abuse, neglect, and civil rights violations documented in all types of residential facilities—government and private, licensed and unlicensed—show that the current federal-state oversight structure is inadequate to protect youth from maltreatment. Comprehensive results of our work will be included in a report to be released next month. This report will provide some options for action that states, federal agencies, and Congress may consider in any restructuring effort. We anticipate our report will also include recommendations for action that federal agencies can implement now under the existing regulatory structure.

Mr. Chairman, this completes my prepared statement. I would be happy to respond to any questions you or other Members of the committee may have.

End Notes

[1] Our review included facilities that provided one or more of the following types of programs: juvenile justice, youth offender, juvenile delinquency, and incorrigibility programs; treatment programs for youth with behavioral, emotional, mental health, and substance abuse issues; homes for pregnant teens; schools for discipline or character education; and therapeutic group homes, such as a home that specializes in supporting and treating youth with severe emotional disorders.

[2] In this report, we use the term *states* to refer collectively to the 50 states plus the District of Columbia and Puerto Rico. We did not survey state education agencies because they generally do not license residential facilities for youth.

[3] In fiscal year 2005, 10 states did not submit reports showing the number of fatalities in residential facilities, 2 states did not submit a report, 7 states did not track facility incident data in a format that could be shared with NCANDS, and 1 state involved in litigation did not report facility data.

[4] For additional information see U.S. Department of Justice *Department of Justice Activities Under the Civil Rights for Institutionalized Persons Act, Fiscal Year 2006*, U.S. Department of Justice (Washington, D.C.: 2007).

[5] According to DOJ officials, the Civil Rights Division has been granted access to HHS's Centers for Medicare and Medicaid Services (CMS) database that contains the annual survey results for CMS oversight of residential facilities.

[6] The survey question was as follows: Which, if any, of the following types of government operated facilities providing residential targeted (child welfare, health mental health, juvenile justice) services for youth are currently exempt from licensing or monitoring in your state by statute or state regulations—state operated facilities? Response options were (a) exempt from licensing by our agency, (b) exempt from routine monitoring by our agency, (c) exempt from both, (d) not exempt from either, (e) no such facility in state, (f) don't know, and (g) no response.

[7] These six states are Arizona, Arkansas, Iowa, Maine, Missouri, and South Carolina. In addition, licensing officials we interviewed in Florida stated that faith-based facilities had the option of being licensed by the state or by a faith-based licensing authority. The survey question was as follows: Which, if any, of the following types of private facilities providing residential targeted services for youth are currently exempt from licensing or routine monitoring in your state by statute or state regulation: Faith-based facilities? (a) exempt from licensure by our agency, (b) exempt from routine monitoring by our agency, (c) exempt from both, (d) not exempt from either, (e) no such facility in state, (f) don't know, and (g) no response.

[8] Across agencies, states most often responded that they did not have private boot camps, ranches, and wilderness camps. Among state juvenile justice agencies, for example, 25 reported having no private boot camps in their state that received government funding, 22 reported having no ranches, and 17 reported having no wilderness camps. Somewhat fewer states reported not having exclusively private boot camps (19), ranches (17), and wilderness camps (14).

[9] Two of the 15 states—Massachusetts and Utah—have a central agency that is responsible for licensing residential facilities. While we did not receive all three surveys from Texas, it also exempts residential schools and academies from licensing.

[10] GAO, *Residential Treatment Programs: Concerns regarding Abuse and Death in Certain Programs for Troubled Youth* GAO-08-146T (Washington, D.C.: October 10, 2007)

[11] For example, HHS's Medicaid program, a federal-state health insurance program for low-income and other specific populations, requires that providers of certain health or mental health services obtain accreditation from an approved accrediting organization to certify that the facility meets standards for safety, quality of care, treatment, and services.

[12] Note: the survey question was as follows: When your agency develops or opens a government-operated residential facility that provides targeted services to youth, is the facility required to meet state standards in any of the following areas? (a) pass inspection of physical plant, (b) provide evidence of safe child care practices, (c) have written procedures for reporting physical or sexual abuse or neglect of youth, (d) meet all staff qualifications requirements, including training, (e) perform staff background checks, (f) meet specified staff-to-child ratios (g) provide evidence of appropriate educational programming, (h) have procedures in place for use of approved seclusion and restraint techniques, and (i) have written suicide prevention plans. A similar question was asked for private facilities.

[13] This derives from Congress' powers under Article I, Section 8 of the U.S. Constitution and provisions of federal law establishing conditions for state grants. Congress, as part of its spending power, can attach conditions to states' receipt of federal funds.

[14] For additional information, see Department of Health and Human Services' Centers for Disease Control Morbidity and Mortality Weekly Report on *Suicide Trends Among Youths and Young Adults, aged 10-24 years—United States, 1990--2004.*

[15] National Center on Institutions and Alternatives. *Juvenile Suicide in Confinement: A National Survey*. February 2004.

[16] This draft notice has been submitted for departmental review and clearance. This rule is being promulgated in response to the Children's Health Act of 2000 (Pub. L. No. 106-310, tit. XXXII, §3208) (amending Title V of the Public Health Service Act)), which requires that public or private non-medical, community-based facilities for children receiving support in any form from any program supported, in whole or part, with funds appropriated under the Children's Health Act, shall protect and promote the rights of each resident of a facility, including the right to be free from any restraint or involuntary seclusion imposed for purposes of discipline or convenience. The statute requires HHS to define in regulation the types of facilities covered by this provision's requirements.

[17] Federal funding was reduced by $1,552,200 among 8 states and territories in 2007.

In: When Abuse and Neglect Occur at Residential... ISBN: 978-1-60876-965-0
Editor: Kirsten S. Madsen pp.21-51

Chapter 2

RESIDENTIAL PROGRAMS: SELECTED CASES OF DEATH, ABUSE AND DECEPTIVE MARKETING*

Gregory D. Kutz

WHY GAO DID THIS STUDY

In October 2007, GAO testified before the Committee regarding allegations of abuse and death in private residential programs across the country such as wilderness therapy programs, boot camps, and boarding schools. GAO also examined selected closed cases where a youth died while enrolled in one of these private programs.

Many cite positive outcomes associated with specific types of residential programs. However, due to continuing concerns about the safety and well-being of youth enrolled in private programs, the Committee requested that GAO (1) identify and examine the facts and circumstances surrounding additional closed cases where a teenager died, was abused, or both, while enrolled in a private program; and (2) identify cases of deceptive marketing or questionable practices in the private residential program industry.

---

* This is an edited, reformatted and augmented version of a U. S. Government Accountability Office publication dated April 2008.

To develop case studies of death and abuse, GAO conducted numerous interviews and examined documents from eight closed cases from 1994 to 2006. GAO used covert testing along with other investigative techniques to identify, for selected cases, deceptive marketing or questionable practices. Specifically, posing as fictitious parents with fictitious troubled teenagers, GAO called 14 programs and related services. GAO did not attempt to evaluate the benefits of private residential programs and its results cannot be projected beyond the specific programs and services that GAO reviewed.

What GAO Found

In the eight closed cases GAO examined, ineffective management and operating practices, in addition to untrained staff, contributed to the death and abuse of youth enrolled in selected programs. The practice of physical restraint also figured prominently in three of the cases. The restraint used for these cases primarily involved one or more staff members physically holding down a youth. See the table below for detailed information related to three of the case studies.

Examples of Case Studies GAO Examined

Sex/age	Date of death/abuse	Case details
Male, 14–18	1994 to 1998	• Victim was restrained over 250 times while attending the program; in at least two cases, restraint lasted over 12 hours
		• One method of restraint included wrapping the victim in a blanket and tying him up
		• Was required to attend the program for 4 years and was held against his will after his 18th birthday
Male, 16	Mar. 1998	• For several weeks, victim complained of chest pain and difficulty breathing
		• Staff forced him to do push-ups and carry cinder blocks as punishment for refusing an assigned task
		• Victim died from an accumulation of infectious pus in his chest

Sex/age	Date of death/abuse	Case details
		• Autopsy found more than 70 injuries on his body, including some from blunt force
Male, 16	Feb. 2006	• Three staff members held the victim facedown to restrain him
		• After 10 minutes of restraint, victim said he could not breathe and was eventually taken to the hospital
		• School was aware victim suffered from asthma, but staff members who restrained him said they were not
		• Victim died of abnormal heartbeat

Source: Records including police reports, legal documents, and state investigative documents.

Posing as fictitious parents with fictitious troubled teenagers, GAO found examples of deceptive marketing and questionable practices in certain industry programs and services. For example, one Montana boarding school told GAO's fictitious parents that their child must apply using an application form before they are admitted. But after a separate call, a program representative e-mailed an acceptance letter for GAO's fictitious child even though an application was never submitted. In another example, the Web site for one referral service states: "We will look at your special situation and help you select the best school for your teen with individual attention." However, GAO called this service three times using three different scenarios related to different fictitious children, and each time the referral agent recommended a Missouri boot camp. Investigative work revealed that the owner of the referral service is married to the owner of the boot camp. GAO also called a program established as a 501(c)(3) charity that advocated a potentially fraudulent tax scheme. The scheme involves the friends and family of a child making tax-deductible "donations" to the charity, which are then credited to an account in the program the child is enrolled in. GAO referred this charity to the Internal Revenue Service for criminal investigation.

Mr. Chairman and Members of the Committee:

Thank you for the opportunity to continue the discussion of private residential programs for troubled youth that we began last fall.[1] In the context of this and our prior testimony, we are using the term residential program to refer to those private entities across the country and abroad that call themselves wilderness therapy programs, therapeutic boarding schools, academies, behavioral modification facilities, ranches, and boot camps, among other names. Many of these programs are privately owned and operated. Private residential programs typically market their services to the parents of troubled teenagers—boys and girls with a variety of addiction, behavioral, and emotional problems—and provide a range of services, including drug and alcohol treatment, confidence building, and psychological counseling for illnesses such as depression and attention deficit disorder. Parents trying to help their troubled child may also seek help from referral services and educational consultants, which generally purport to assess the needs of the child and recommend an appropriate program.

Many cite positive outcomes associated with specific types of residential programs. However, in our previous testimony, we identified thousands of allegations of abuse, some of which resulted in death, at residential programs across the country and in American-owned and American- operated facilities abroad. We also examined 10 closed civil or criminal cases where a teenager died while enrolled in a private program and found significant evidence of ineffective management in most of the 10 cases, with program leaders neglecting the needs of program participants and staff. This ineffective management compounded the negative consequences of (and sometimes directly resulted in) the hiring of untrained staff; a lack of adequate nourishment for enrolled children; and reckless or negligent operating practices, including a lack of adequate equipment.

Due to your continuing concern about the safety and well-being of youth enrolled in private residential programs, and to assist the Committee in its consideration of the need for federal legislation in this area, you requested that we (1) identify and examine the facts and circumstances surrounding additional closed cases where a teenager died, was abused, or both, while enrolled in a private program; and (2) identify cases of deceptive marketing or other questionable practices in the private residential program industry.

To identify case studies, we reviewed numerous closed criminal or civil cases in which a court or state agency was asked to decide whether a private residential program was responsible for the death or abuse of an enrolled teenager. We also reviewed administrative cases where state agencies made rulings regarding the death or abuse of a teenager. When identifying cases, we specifically excluded public programs such as state-sponsored foster programs, juvenile justice programs for delinquent youth, or programs that exclusively treat psychological disorders or substance abuse in a hospital setting. We also excluded cases related to the programs we examined for our

October 10, 2007, testimony. We focused on deaths or instances of abuse between the years 1994 and 2006 to illustrate the long-standing issues presented by private residential programs. We limited our cases to closed criminal cases and, thus, did not include ongoing cases from the last several years. We selected eight cases—four cases of death and four cases of abuse—based on several factors including the victim's age, the program location, the type of program the victim attended, and the date of death or abuse. We then examined, in more detail, the facts and circumstances of the case. To validate the facts and circumstances, and to the extent possible, we conducted interviews with related parties, including current and former program staff and officials, attorneys and law enforcement officials involved in the cases, and the parents of the victims. Further, we reviewed available documentation to support the facts of each case including, but not limited to, marketing materials, police reports, autopsy reports, and state agency oversight reviews and investigations.

To identify cases of deceptive marketing or other questionable practices in the private residential program industry, we used a variety of approaches and investigative techniques. Posing as fictitious parents with fictitious troubled children, our undercover investigators made telephone calls to a nonrepresentative selection of 10 private residential programs and 4 referral services. Like legitimate parents with troubled teenagers, we identified these programs and referral services through Internet searches and magazine advertisements. To assess the accuracy and reasonableness of the information we obtained during each undercover call, we performed additional follow-up work that included, but was not limited to, making additional undercover calls; comparing the information we received with other marketing information provided by the program; reviewing relevant laws, regulations, and trade organization statements; performing announced, agreed upon site visits (i.e., not undercover); and speaking with cognizant state and federal officials, including the Internal Revenue Service (IRS).

We performed our work from November 2007 through April 2008 in accordance with the quality standards for investigations set forth by the President's Council on Integrity and Efficiency. As we noted in our prior testimony, it is important to emphasize that residential programs are intended to help youth with serious problems, including life-threatening addictions and diseases. We did not attempt to evaluate the benefits of residential programs in dealing with these serious problems. In addition, it is not possible to generalize the results of our investigation as applying to all residential programs, whether privately or publicly funded, or referral services and educational consultants and others in the residential program industry. Moreover, it is difficult to develop a picture of the overall industry, its practices, and efforts to oversee it. For example, while states often regulate publicly funded programs, a number of states do not license or otherwise regulate certain types of private programs. GAO is completing a more comprehensive review of state and federal oversight of residential programs and expects to issue a report soon.

Summary of Investigation

In the eight closed cases we examined, ineffective management and operating practices, in addition to untrained staff, contributed to the death and abuse of youth enrolled in selected programs. In the most egregious cases of death and abuse, the cases exposed problems with the entire operation of the program. The practice of physical restraint also figured prominently in three of the cases. The restraint used for these cases primarily involved one or more staff members physically holding down a youth. Examples of some case studies follow:

- A 16 year-old male who suffered from asthma and chronic bronchitis complained of chest pain and had difficulty breathing for several weeks. Staff at the Arizona boot camp he was attending punished him for refusing to do an assigned task and forced him to do push-ups and carry cinder blocks; meanwhile, a program nurse told him the breathing problems were "in your head." In March 1998, the victim died from an accumulation of infectious pus in his chest, and an autopsy found more than 70 injuries, including blunt-force injuries, on his body—indicating he had been physically abused before his death.
- A teenage male was required to attend a behavior modification program in New Jersey for 4 years, and was held against his will after he turned 18. Records show that the victim was restrained more than 250 times while attending the program. Incident reports filed by program staff document that after he had turned 18, the victim was restrained on 26 separate days, with at least two restraints lasting more than 12 hours. Restraints were imposed any time he showed reluctance to participate in the program, and for other reasons; on one occasion, he said he was wrapped in a blanket and tied up after attempting to escape the program.

- In February 2006, a 16-year-old male with a history of asthma became unresponsive while being restrained at a Pennsylvania treatment facility. He died 3 hours later in a hospital. An investigation into the death found that the facility had documentation of the victim's history of asthma, and that its training manual for restraint procedures cautioned against the risk of decreased oxygen intake during restraints for youth with asthma. However, all three staff members involved in the restraint that led to the victim's death told investigators that they were unaware of any medical conditions that needed to be considered when restraining the victim.

In three of the eight cases we examined, the victim was placed in the program by the state or in consultation with state authorities.

Posing as fictitious parents with fictitious troubled teenagers, we also found examples of deceptive marketing and questionable practices in the private residential program industry. Deceptive marketing included potential fraud, false statements, and misleading representations related to a range of issues including tax deductions, education, and admissions policies. We also found undisclosed conflicts of interest. Examples of deceptive marketing included the following:

- One Montana boarding school told us that parents must submit an application form in order for their child to be considered for admission in the program. However, after a separate call by a fictitious parent, a program representative e-mailed us that our fictitious daughter had been approved for admission into the program and subsequently sent an acceptance letter. This acceptance into the school was based on a 30-minute telephone conversation. We did not fill out any application form.
- The Web site for one referral service we called says: "We will look at your special situation and help you select the best school for your teen with individual attention." However, we called this service three times using three different scenarios related to different fictitious children, and each time the referral agent recommended a Missouri boot camp. Investigative work revealed that the owner of the referral service is married to the owner of the boot camp, but this relationship was never disclosed during the call, raising the issue of conflict of interest.
- The representative for a 501(c)(3) foundation suggested our fictitious parents take advantage of a fund-raising approach that is potentially a

fraudulent tax scheme. The representative said that this "popular" option would allow friends, family, business acquaintances, churches, and other organizations to make tax-deductible donations that would then be credited to our fictitious child's tuition in a private program. After we briefed an IRS official on the representation by this foundation, he told us that the foundation is potentially committing tax fraud and that those who obtain tax benefits for donations in the suggested manner may be responsible for back taxes, as well as penalties and interest.

A link to selected audio clips from these calls is available at: http://www.gao.gov/media/video/gao-08-713t/

BACKGROUND

Since the early 1990s, state agencies and private companies have set up hundreds of residential programs and facilities in the United States. Many of these programs are intended to provide a less restrictive alternative to incarceration or hospitalization for youth who may require intervention to address emotional or behavioral challenges. A wide array of government or private entities, including government agencies and faith-based organizations, operate these programs. Some residential programs advertise themselves as focusing on a specific client type, such as those with substance abuse disorders or suicidal tendencies.

As we reported in our October 2007 testimony, no federal laws define what constitutes a residential program, nor are there any standard, commonly recognized definitions for specific types of programs. For our purposes, we define programs based on the characteristics we have identified during our work. For example:

- Wilderness therapy programs place youth in different natural environments, including forests, mountains, and deserts. According to wilderness therapy program material, these settings are intended to remove the "distractions" and "temptations" of modern life from teens, forcing them to focus on themselves and their relationships. These programs are typically 28 days in length at a minimum, but parents can continue to enroll their child for longer at an additional cost.

- Boot camps are residential programs in which strict discipline and regime are dominant principles. Many boot camps emphasize behavioral modification elements, and some military-style boot camps also emphasize uniformity and austere living conditions. Boot camps might be included as part of a wilderness therapy school or therapeutic boarding, but many boot camps exist independently. These programs are offered year-round and some summer programs last up to 3 months.
- Boarding schools (also called academies) are generally advertised as providing academic education beyond the survival skills a wilderness therapy program might teach. These programs frequently enroll youth whose parents force them to attend against their will. The schools can include fences and other security measures to ensure that youth do not leave without permission. While these programs advertise year-round education, the length of stay varies for each student; contracts can require stays of up to 21 months or more.
- Ranch programs typically emphasize remoteness and large, open spaces available on program property. Many ranch programs advertise the therapeutic value of ranch-related work. These programs also generally provide an opportunity for youth to help care for horses and other animals. Although we could not determine the length of a typical stay at ranch programs, they operate year-round and take students for as long as 18 months.

See appendix I for further information about the location of various types of residential programs across the United States. In addition to these programs, the industry includes a variety of ancillary services. These include referral services and educational consultants to assist parents in selecting a program, along with transport services to pick up a youth and bring him or her to the program location. Parents frequently use a transport service if their child is unwilling to attend the program.

Private programs generally charge high tuition costs. For example, one wilderness program stated that their program costs over $13,000 for 28 days. In addition to tuition costs, these programs frequently charge additional fees for enrollment, uniforms, medical care, supplemental therapy, and other services—all of which vary by program and can add up to thousands of extra dollars. Costs for ancillary services vary. The cost for transport services depends on a number of factors, including distance traveled and the means of transportation. Referral services do not charge parents fees, but educational consultants do and typically charge thousands of dollars. Financial and loan services are also available to assist parents in covering the expense of residential programs and are often advertised by programs and referral services. See appendix II for further information about the cost of residential programs across the United States.

There are no federal oversight laws—including reporting requirements—pertaining specifically to private residential programs, referral services, educational consultants, or transportation services, with one limited exception. The U.S. Department of Health and Human Services oversees psychiatric residential treatment facilities (PRTFs) receiving Medicaid funds. In order to be eligible to receive funds under Medicaid, PRTFs must abide by regulations that govern the use of restraint and seclusion techniques on patients. They are also required to report serious incidents to both state Medicaid agencies and, unless prohibited by state law, state Protection and Advocacy agencies. In addition, the regulations require PRTFs to report patient deaths to the Centers for Medicare and Medicaid Services Regional Office.[2]

CASES OF DEATH AND ABUSE AT SELECTED RESIDENTIAL PROGRAMS

In the eight closed cases we examined, ineffective management and operating practices, in addition to untrained staff, contributed to the death and abuse of youth enrolled in selected programs. Furthermore, two cases of death were very similar to cases from our October 2007 testimony, in that staff ignored the serious medical complaints of youth until it was too late. The practice of physical restraint figured prominently in three of the cases. The restraint used for these cases primarily involved one or more staff members physically holding down a youth. Ineffective operating practices led to the most egregious cases of death and abuse, as the cases exposed problems with the entire operation of the program. Specifically, the failure of program leaders to ensure that appropriate policies and procedures were in place to deal with the serious problems of youth; ineffective management practices that led to questionable therapeutic or operational practices; and the failure of the program to share information about enrolled youth with the staff members who were attending to them created the environments that resulted in abuse and death. Moreover, in cases involving abuse, the abuse was systemic in the program and not limited to the incident discussed in our case studies. In three of the eight cases we examined, the victim was placed in the program by the state or in consultation with state authorities.[3]

See table 1 for a summary of the cases of death we examined.

See table 2 for a summary of the cases of abuse we examined. For reporting purposes, we continue the numbering of case studies in this table, starting with five.

The following three narratives describe selected cases in further detail.

Case 3 (Death)

The victim, who died in 2005, was a 12-year-old male. Documents obtained from the Texas Department of Family and Protective Services indicate that the victim had a troubled family background. He was taken into state care along with his siblings at the age of 6. According to child protective service workers who visited the family's home, the victim and his siblings were found unsupervised and without electricity, water, or food. Some of the children were huddled over a space heater, which was connected to a neighbor's house by extension cord, in order to keep warm. As a ward of the state, the victim spent several years in various foster placements and youth programs before being placed in a private residential treatment center in August 2005. The program advertised itself as a "unique facility" that specialized in services for boys with learning disabilities and behavioral or emotional issues. The victim's caretakers chose to place him in this program because he was emotionally disturbed. Records indicate that he was covered by Medicaid.

On the evening of his death, the victim refused to take a shower and was ordered to sit on an outside porch. According to police reports, the victim began to bang his head repeatedly against the concrete floor of the porch, leading a staff member to drag him away from the porch and place him in a "lying basket restraint" for his own protection. During this restraint, the 4 feet 91/2 inch tall, 87-pound boy was forced to lie on his stomach with his arms crossed under him as the staff member, a muscular male 5 feet 10 inches tall, held him still.

Table 1. Summary of Eight Closed Cases (Four Deaths)

Case	Victim information	Program Attended	Date of death	Cause of death	Case details
1	Male, 16, California resident	Arizona boot camp	March 1998	Empyema (accumulation of infectious pus in the chest)	• Victim suffered from asthma and chronic bronchitis
					• For a period of several weeks, victim complained of chest pain and difficulty breathing, but a program nurse said that his breathing problems were in his head
					• Staff punished him for refusing an assigned task, and forced him to do push-ups and carry cinder blocks
					• Victim eventually became unresponsive, at which point staff finally realized that his condition required medical attention
					• Victim was declared dead at a hospital
					• Autopsy found more than 70 injuries, including some from blunt force, on hisbody,
					• indicating that the victim had been physically abused before his death

Case	Victim information	Program Attended	Date of death	Cause of death	Case details
2	Male, 14, Texas resident	Texas wilderness therapy program	Sept. 2004	Cardiopulmonary Arrest	• Victim's hiking group became lost and spent several unforeseen hours in temperatures that reached 98 degrees (a reported heat index of near 105 degrees)
					• During the hike, victim stopped and complained that he was too hot and tired and refused to go on, but he was encouraged to continue
					• Victim said he didn't feel well and was dizzy, then stumbled and fell
					• Staff thought he was "faking"
					• When victim began to vomit, staff rolled him on his side
					• Victim stopped breathing and was later pronounced dead
					• Died on federal land
3	Male, 12, Texas resident	Texas residential treatment center	Dec. 2005	Suffocation	• Victim was angry and started banging his head against the ground
					• A 5 feet 10 inch, muscular staff member placed the 87-pound victim into a facedown restraint

Table 1. (Continued)

Case	Victim information	Program Attended	Date of death	Cause of death	Case details
					• Several witnesses claimed they saw the staff member lying across the back of the victim
					• Victim complained he couldn't breathe and eventually became unresponsive, at which point the staff member removed the restraint
					• After the victim had lain unresponsive for about a minute, the staff member rolled him over and found that he was pale
					• Attempts to revive victim failed
4	Male, 16, Pennsylvania resident	Pennsylvania psychiatric residential treatment center	Feb. 2006	Abnormal heartbeat	• Victim was placed under "intense observation" for attempting to run away from the program
					• Victim was ordered to put the hood of his sweatshirt down so that staff could see his face, but victim refused
					• Three staff members brought the victim to another room and placed him in restraint face down

Case	Victim information	Program Attended	Date of death	Cause of death	Case details
					• After 10 minutes of the restraint, victim complained that he couldn't breathe
					• Despite staff attempts to make the victim more comfortable, victim became unresponsive
					• Victim died at the hospital 3 hours later from an abnormal heartbeat
					• Program was aware victim suffered from asthma, but staff members who restrained the victim claimed they were not aware of this

Source: Records including police reports, legal documents, and state investigative documents.

Table 2. Summary of Eight Closed Cases (Four Abuse)

Case	Victim information	Program attended	Date(s) of abuse	Case details
5	Male, 14-18, New York resident	New Jersey residential behavior modification program	1994 to 1998	• Victim and parents were interviewed separately by staff during his first visit to the program
				• Victim encountered 6 hours of intense questioning during which he felt forced to confess to activities he says he did not take part in, such as illegal drug use and sex
				• Victim was restrained more than 250 times while attending the program; in at least two cases restraint lasted longer than 12 hours
				• One method of restraint included wrapping the victim in a blanket and tying him up
				• Victim was required to attend the program for 4 years and was held against his will after his 18th birthday

Table 2. (Continued)

Case	Victim information	Program attended	Date(s) of abuse	Case details
6	Male, 17, Washington resident	Mississippi faith-based academy and boot camp	April 1999	• Victim jumped off a building and broke his left arm; the bone of his arm was exposed, but he was not given medical attention for 2 weeks
				• Students and staff harassed the victim, with some boys subjecting him to physical abuse
				• On one occasion, victim was beaten unconscious by staff and other students
				• On another occasion, a staff member's pit bull bit the victim in the crotch
				• Victim had previously attended boarding school in case 7
7	Male, 15, California resident	Utah boarding school	Nov. 2004	• Victim was verbally abused and punched, kicked, and slapped by other students, under direction of one of the school's owners
				• Victim was hit and pushed down stairs by the same school owner

Table 2. (Continued)

Case	Victim information	Program attended	Date(s) of abuse	Case details
				• On multiple occasions throughout his stay in the school, victim was locked in a bathroom and a closet and forced to sleep on a shelf as punishment
8	Male, 14, California resident	Colorado boarding school	May 2006	• Staff member assaulted victim by grabbing him by the arm, pushing him into a stairwell, and slamming his face into a wall
				• Victim's face was visibly bruised, including a black eye
				• Victim was forced to kneel on the floor for hours with his knees at the point where the floor meets the wall and his nose touching the wall

Source: Records including police reports, legal documents, and state investigative documents.

Some of the children who witnessed the restraint said they saw the staff member lying across the victim's back. During the restraint, the victim fought against the staff member and yelled at him to stop. The staff member told police that the victim complained that he could not breathe, but added that children "always say that they cannot breathe during a restraint." According to police reports, after about 10 minutes of forced restraint, the staff member observed that the victim had calmed down and was no longer fighting back. The staff member slowly released the restraint and asked the victim if he wanted a jacket. The victim did not respond. The staff member told police he interpreted the victim's silence as an unwillingness to talk due to anger about the restraint. He said he waited for a minute while the victim lay silently on the ground. When the victim did not respond to his question a second time, he tapped the victim on the shoulder and rolled him over. The staff member observed that the victim was pale and could not detect a pulse. All efforts to revive the victim failed, and he was declared dead at a nearby hospital.

When the staff member demonstrated his restraint technique for the police, they found that his technique violated the restraint policies of the program. These policies prohibited staff from placing any pressure on the back of a person being restrained. The report added that this staff member was reprimanded for injuring a youth in 2002 as a result of improper restraint. After this incident, program administrators banned the staff member from participating in restraints for 1 month. The reprimand issued by program administrators over this incident noted that the staff member had actually trained other staff members in performing restraints, making the matter more serious. The police reports also cite one of the staff member's performance evaluations that noted that he had problems with his temper. According to the reports, one of the youth in the program said the staff member could become agitated when putting youth in restraint.

Although the Texas Department of Family and Protective Services alleged that the victim's death was due to physical abuse, the official certificate of death stated that it was an accident and a grand jury declined to press charges against the staff member performing the restraint. However, the victim's siblings obtained a civil settlement against the program and the staff member for an undisclosed amount. The program remained open until May 2006, when a 12-year-old boy drowned on a bike outing with the program. According to records from law enforcement, child protection workers, and the program, the boy fell into the water of a rain-swollen creek and was sucked into a culvert. He died after several weeks on life support. The Texas Department of Family and Protective Services cited negligent staff supervision in its review of this second death and revoked the program's license to operate as a residential treatment center. However, the program's directors also ran a summer camp for children with learning disabilities and social disorders licensed by the Texas Department of State Health Services, until they resigned from their positions in March 2008.

Case 4 (Death)

The victim was 16 years old when he died, in February 2006, at a private psychiatric residential treatment facility in Pennsylvania for boys with behavioral or emotional problems. He was a large boy—6 feet 1 inch in height and weighing about 250 pounds—and suffered from bipolar disorder and asthma. The cost for placement in this facility was primarily paid for by Medicaid.

According to state investigative documents we obtained, the victim was placed in intensive observation after he attempted to run away. As part of the intensive observation, he was forced to sit in a chair in the hallway of the facility and was restricted from participating in some activities with other residents. On the day of his death, staff allowed the victim to participate in arts, crafts, and games with the other youth, but would not let him leave the living area to attend other recreational activities. Instead, staff told the victim that he would have to return to his chair in the hallway. In addition, staff told him that he would have to move his chair so that he could not see the television in another room. The victim complied, moving his chair out of view of the television, but put up the hood of his sweatshirt and turned his back toward the staff. The staff ordered him to take down his hood but he refused. When one of the staff walked up to him and pulled his hood down, the victim jumped out of his chair and made a threatening posture with his fists, saying he did not want to be touched. The staff member and two coworkers then brought the victim to another room and held him facedown on the floor with his arms pulled up behind his back. The victim struggled against the restraint, yelling and trying to kick the three staff members holding him down. After about 10 minutes, the victim became limp and started breathing heavily. He complained that he was having difficulties breathing. One staff member unzipped his sweatshirt and loosened the collar of his shirt, but rather than improve, the victim became unresponsive. The staff called emergency services and began CPR. The victim was taken by ambulance to a hospital, where he died a little more than 3 hours later. In the victim's autopsy report his death was ruled accidental, as caused by asphyxia and an abnormal heartbeat (cardiac dysrhythmia).

Following the victim's death, an investigation by the Pennsylvania Department of Health found that the policies and procedures for youth under intense observation do not prohibit them from watching television, nor do they require that youth keep their face visible to staff at all times. The investigation also found that the facility had documentation of the victim's history of asthma, and that its training manual for restraint procedures cautioned against the risk of decreased oxygen intake during restraints for children with asthma. However, all three staff members involved in the restraint told investigators that they were unaware of any medical conditions that needed to be considered when restraining the victim. In addition, the investigation found that the facility did not provide timely training on the appropriate and safe use of restraint. The state's Protection and Advocacy organization, Pennsylvania Protection & Advocacy, Inc. (PP&A), conducted its own investigation of the facility and found that staff members inappropriately restrained children in lieu of appropriate behavioral interventions, which resulted in neglect and abuse. Of the 45 residents interviewed by PP&A investigators, 29 said that staff at the facility subjected them to restraints. The residents reported that the restraints could last as long as 90 minutes and caused breathing difficulties. They also stated that staff often placed their knees on residents' backs and necks during restraints. One resident reported that the blood vessels in his eyes "popped" during a restraint. Another resident said that his nose hit the ground during the restraint, causing him to choke on his own blood. Further, some of the residents reported that staff provoked them and that staff did not make any effort to de-escalate the provocations before implementing a restraint.

No criminal charges were filed in regard to the victim's death. The victim's mother filed a civil suit over her son's death against the facility, which is currently pending. Her son's death was not the only fatal incident at this facility. Only 2 months before the victim's death, in December 2005, a 17-year-old boy collapsed at the facility after a physical education class, and later died at a nearby hospital. His death was attributed to an enlarged heart. This facility remains open.

Case 5 (Abuse)

This abuse victim was sent to a private drug and addiction treatment program in July 1994 at the age of 14. He was attending public school in the major metropolitan area where his family lived. The abuse victim told us that he had problems at school, including poor grades, truancy, a fight with other students, and that he had been suspended. After the victim was questioned by police about an assault on a girl at his school, a family friend with ties to the behavior modification program recommended the program to the victim's parents. According to the victim, his first visit to the school turned into an intense intake session where he was interviewed by two program patients. Although the victim denied using drugs, the interviewers insisted that he was not being honest. After about 6 hours of questioning, the victim told the interviewers what he thought they wanted to hear—that he was smoking pot, did cocaine, and cut school to get high—so that he could end the interview. The interviewers used these statements to convince the victim's parents to sign him into the program for immediate intervention and treatment. He ended up staying in the program for the next 4 years—even after he turned 18 and was held against his will.

According to program records, the program's part-time psychiatrist did not examine or diagnose him until he had been in the program for 14 days. This lack of psychological care continued, as program records indicate he was examined by the psychiatrist only four times during his entire stay. He was restrained more than 250 times while in the program, with at least 46 restraints lasting one hour or longer. The victim said some restraints were applied by a group of four or five staff members and fellow patients.

According to the victim, they held him on his back, with one person holding his head and one person holding each limb. These restraints were imposed whenever the victim showed any reluctance to do what he was told, or, the victim told us, for doing some things without first obtaining permission from program staff. On one occasion, while he was staying with a host family and other patients, he attempted to escape from the program. The victim claims that they restrained him by wrapping him in a blanket and tying him up. According to the victim, when he turned 18, he submitted a request to leave the program but his request was denied because he had not followed the proper procedure and was a danger to himself. For expressing his desire to leave the program, he was stripped of all progress he had made to that point, and was prevented from further advancing until the program director decided he was be eligible. Incident reports filed by program staff document that after he had turned 18, the victim was restrained on 26 separate days, with at least two restraints lasting more than 12 hours.

According to program rules, failure of the parents to follow program rules and fully support and participate in the program would jeopardize their son's treatment and progress and put him at risk of expulsion. Having been led to believe that the program was the only way to help him overcome his alleged addictions and problems, his family complied with the program's demands. Moreover, the program required parents and siblings over age 8 to attend twice weekly group therapy meetings. According to the victim, these meetings lasted for many hours, sometimes stretching into the early morning. He added that when the victim's father refused to attend the therapy meetings for fear of losing his job, the program told him to quit. When he would not quit his job or miss work to attend the meetings, the victim said that the program convinced his mother to leave her husband. After his parents separated, the program would not allow the victim to have contact with his father. The victim said that the program never told the victim's family that all the drug tests they performed on him returned negative results, including the initial tests done when he entered the program.

In February 1998, the State of New Jersey terminated the program's participation in the Medicaid program, holding that the program did not qualify as a children's partial care mental health program because of its noncompliance with client rights standards and its failure to meet various staff requirements, such as staff-to-client ratios and requisite education and experience levels for staff. The program subsequently closed in November 1998, citing financial problems. About a year later, in September 1999, an administrative law judge rejected an appeal by the program to overrule the state's termination of its Medicaid participation. The judge noted in his decision that the program effectively operated as a full-time residential facility. Moreover, he noted that all group staff at the program were either current or former patients, and only two members of the program staff met the educational requirements to qualify as direct- care professionals.

The victim filed a civil lawsuit against the program, director, and a psychiatrist, which resulted in a $3.75 million settlement. Other civil suits filed by former patients included one patient who was committed to the program at the age of 13 and spent 13 years in the program. This patient reached a similar settlement against the program, director, and psychiatrists for the sum of $6.5 million. In addition, a third former patient secured a $4.5 million settlement against the program, director, and psychiatrists.

Deceptive Marketing and Questionable Practices in Selected Programs and Services

Posing as fictitious parents with fictitious troubled teenagers, we found examples of deceptive marketing and questionable practices related to 10 private residential programs and 4 referral services. The most egregious deceptive marketing practices related to tax incentives and health insurance reimbursement, and were intended to make the high price of the programs appear more manageable for our fictitious parents. We also found examples of false statements and misleading representations related to a range of issues including education and admissions, as well as undisclosed conflicts of interest. In addition, we identified examples of questionable practices related to the health of youth enrolled in programs and the method of convincing reluctant parents to enroll their children. Although general consumer protection laws apply to these programs and services, there are no federal laws or regulations on marketing content and practices specific to the residential program industry.

A link to selected audio clips from these calls is available at: http://www.gao.gov/media/video/gao-08-713t/. See table 3 for a selection of representations made by programs and referral agents.

Case 1: One of our fictitious parents called this foundation pretending to be a parent who could not afford the cost of a residential program for his child. A representative of the foundation explained that their "most popular" method of fund-raising involved the friends and relatives of the enrolled youth making tax-deductible donations to the foundation, which in turn credited 90 percent of these "donations" specifically to pay for tuition in a program the child was attending. The foundation assigns a code number to each child, which parents ensure is listed on the donation checks. The representative also provided a fund-raising packet by mail that instructs the parents of troubled teens: "You are able to contact family, friends, business acquaintances, affiliates, churches, and professional/fraternal organizations that you know. Don't forget corporate matching funds opportunities from your employer too." The packet also included two template letters to send in soliciting the funds. According to an IRS official with the Tax Exempt and Governmental Entities Division, this practice is inappropriate and represents potential tax fraud on the part of the foundation. Furthermore, those who claim inappropriate deductions in this fashion would be responsible for back taxes, as well as penalties and interest.

Based on this information, we referred this nonprofit foundation to the IRS for criminal investigation.

Table 3. Cases of Deceptive Marketing and Questionable Practices

Source	Representation	Comments
1. 501(c)(3) charity foundation	Foundation representative described a funding mechanism whereby (1) parents solicit friends, relatives, and others to make financial donations to the foundation and have them specify on their donation checks a numbered code representing the child; (2) the foundation tracks the donation amount on behalf of the child, then deducts an administrative fee and pays the program the remaining donation amount on behalf of that child; and (3) friends and family deduct the charitable donations on their tax return	An IRS official told us that the foundation is potentially committing tax fraud and that individuals who follow the program's recommendation may be responsible for back taxes, as well as penalties and interest for taking an improper charitable deduction
2. Montana boarding school	Program representatives told one fictitious parent that an application form must be filled out before a child is admitted to the boarding school	After a call to this program by a different fictitious parent, we received an acceptance letter for our fictitious child even though we never applied for admission
3. Texas wilderness program	Program representative stated that earth science credits earned in the program are "fully transferable" and that other institutions "can't deny" the credit	Education credits can be denied by schools for any reason and are not intrinsically transferable
4. Texas wilderness program (same as case no. 3)	Program representative said that the program will provide parents with a detailed bill after their child completes the program and that health insurance companies will reimburse expenses	Representatives for both a health care insurer and a behavioral health company told us that parents who follow this advice run a real risk of not being reimbursed, especially if the health insurance company requires pre-approval of counseling or other mental health services

Table 3 (Continued)

Source	Representation	Comments
5. Texas wilderness program (same as case nos. 3 and 4)	Program representative said a trade organization, the National Association of Therapeutic Schools and Programs (NATSAP), "absolutely" performs inspections of the program	NATSAP does not perform inspections of its member programs
Source	**Representation**	**Comments**
6. Referral service "A"	Referral agent stated that behavioral modification schools are "specialty schools" and that tuition costs are tax deductible under Section 213 of the Internal Revenue Tax code	The two programs recommended by the referral agent do not appear to meet the requirements of IRS regulations for special schools; according to an IRS authority on Section 213 with whom we spoke, this is questionable tax advice and parents should consult a tax advisor
7. Referral service "A"	The referral agent warned our fictitious parent that his wife might "freak out" about sending her daughter to a boarding school, and stated: "I want you to tell her it's a college prep boarding school… if she thinks that you want to send her daughter to a place where there are drug addicts and people that are all screwed up, she will look at you and say 'no way'"	In order to secure the business of our fictitious parent, the referral agent gave us questionable ethical advice
8. Referral service "B"	Referral agent stated that the program he recommended "feed[s] the child a whole-grain diet" and that along with exercise and rest, "the bipolar, the depression, those kind of things, they just go away after awhile"	Although diet and sleep may be beneficial, there was no discussion during the call for a health care provider to confirm the child's diagnosis of bipolar disorder or depression and whether to continue medication
9. Referral service "B"	Web site for this referral service states: "We will look at your special situation and help you select the best school for your teen with individual attention"	Referral agents recommended the same Missouri boot camp to three different fictitious parents with three fictitious children having very different problems; the referral service is owned by the husband of the woman who owns the Missouri boot camp, but the conflict of interest was not disclosed
10. Referral services "A" and "C"	When investigators called the phone number of referral service "A" the receptionist answered the call using the name of referral service "C"	Referral services "A" and "C" represent themselves as separate entities, with separate names, Web sites, phone numbers, and magazine advertisements, suggesting that they provide objective advice

Source: GAO.

Case 2: The program representative at a Montana boarding school told our fictitious parent that they must submit an application form before their child can be accepted to the school. However, after a separate undercover call made to this school by one of our fictitious parents, the program representative e-mailed us stating that our fictitious daughter had been approved for admission into the program and subsequently sent an acceptance letter. The acceptance letter stated that our fictitious child "has been approved for our school here in Montana." This admission was based entirely on one 30-minute telephone conversation, in which our fictitious parent described his daughter as a 13-year-old who takes the psychotropic medication Risperdal, attends weekly therapy sessions, has bipolar disorder, and been diagnosed with Reactive Attachment Disorder. We did not fill out an application form for the school. Moreover, this program had previously recommended that our fictitious parents seek advice from the 501(c)(3)foundation discussed in Case 1 to help finance the cost of the program. It appears that parents do not have assurance about the integrity of the admissions process at this boarding school.

Case 4: One fictitious parent asked the representative for a Texas wilderness therapy program whether there was any possibility that a health insurance company would cover the cost of the program. The representative replied that, at the completion of the program, the bookkeeper for the program would generate an itemized statement of billable charges that could be submitted to an insurance company for reimbursement. She emphasized that we should not call ahead of time to seek pre-approval, because then we would be "up the creek." She added that this was "just the way insurance companies like it" and stated that health insurance companies reimburse "quite a bit." She gave an example of one insurance company that reimbursed for over $11,000—almost the entire cost of the 28-day wilderness program. Representatives for both a health care insurer and a behavioral health company told us that parents who follow this advice run a real risk of not being reimbursed, especially if the health insurance company requires pre-approval of counseling or other mental health services. In this case, our fictitious parent was being led into believing that a large portion of the tuition for the program would be covered by health insurance even if pre-approval for the charges was not obtained in writing in advance of the services.

Case 6: One referral agent we called stated that behavioral modification schools are "specialty schools" and that tuition costs are tax deductible under Section 213 of the Internal Revenue Tax code. The referral agent also stated that transportation costs related to bringing our fictitious child to and from the school were tax deductible under this section. However, the two programs recommended by the referral service do not appear to meet the requirements of IRS regulations for special schools. Our review of Section 213 of the Internal

Revenue Tax code shows that it relates to medical expenses and specifies that, if medical expenses and transportation for treatment exceed 7.5 percent of a taxpayer's adjusted gross income, the excess costs can be deducted on Schedule A of IRS Form 1040. Even if these expenses were deductible under this section, only expenses above 7.5 percent of the adjusted gross income would be deductible, rather than the full amount as suggested by the referral agent. An IRS authority on Section 213 with whom we spoke stated that the referral service provided us with questionable tax advice and that parents should consult a tax advisor before attempting to claim a deduction under this section. Parents improperly taking this deduction could be responsible for back taxes, as well as penalties and interest.

Case 9: On its Web site, referral service "B" invites parents to call a toll-free number and states: "We will look at your special situation and help you select the best school for your teen with individual attention." Our undercover investigators called this referral service pretending to be three separate fictitious parents and described three separate fictitious children to the agents who answered the phone. Despite these three different scenarios, we found the referral service recommended the same residential program all three times—a Missouri boot camp. Our investigation into this referral service revealed that the owner of the referral service is the husband of the boot camp owner. This relationship, was not disclosed to our fictitious parents during our telephone calls, which raises the issue of a potential conflict of interest. It appears that parents who call this referral service will not receive the objective advice they expect based on marketing information on the Web site.

Mr. Chairman and Members of the Committee, this concludes my statement. We would be pleased to answer any questions that you may have at this time.

Appendix I: Private Residential Program Locations

In our examination of case studies for this testimony and our prior testimony, we found that the victims of death and abuse came from across the country and attended programs that were similarly located in numerous states. Figure 1 contains a map indicating where victims lived and the location of the program they attended.

Private residential programs are located nationwide and rely heavily on the Internet for their marketing. Although Web sites list 48 of the 50 states where parents can find various types of programs, we found that they do not list programs in Nebraska and South Dakota, nor do they indicate the existence of programs in the District of Columbia. Notably, we did not find Web sites that list states with boot camps but instead instruct parents to call for locations and details. Figure 2 illustrates the types of programs and the states in which they are located, excluding boot camps.

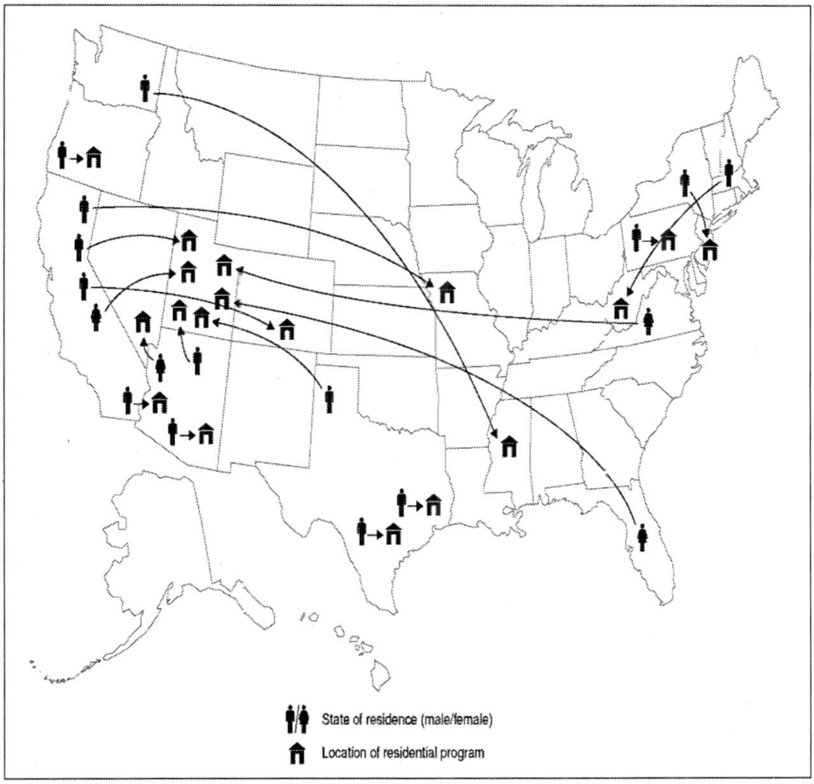

Source: GAO.

Note: The icons in figure 1 represent the state of residence for each case study victim and the state in which each residential program is located. The icons do not reflect specific geographic locations within states.

Figure1. Private Residential Programs Nationwide

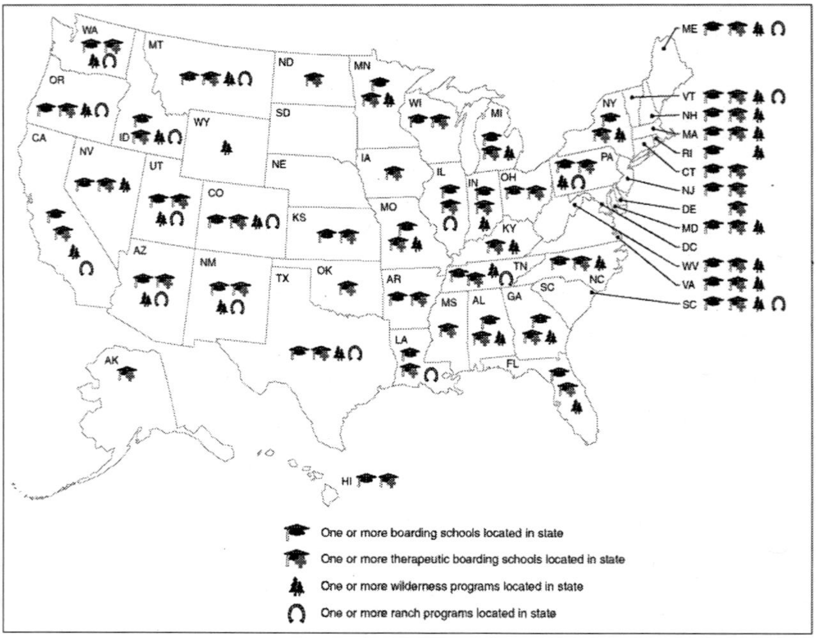

Source: GAO analysis of information available on referral service Web sites.

Figure 2. Private Residential Programs Nationwide

APPENDIX II: COST OF PRIVATE RESIDENTIAL PROGRAMS

According to program and service representatives with whom we spoke, the basic cost could be discounted. For example, one program told us if parents paid for a full year upfront, they would be given a $200-per-month discount. This does not include fees by transport services for taking a child to a program. Moreover, although program and service representatives quoted these as basic program costs, they also mentioned additional one-time charges, such as an enrollment fee that can be as much as $4,600, uniform costs, or other items such as supplies. In addition, some programs charge extra for therapy, including one-on-one therapy.

Our undercover calls to selected programs revealed that most private programs charge a high tuition for their services. Table 4 contains information related to the high cost of these programs based these phone calls.

Table 4. Basic Monthly Costs of Programs

No.	Type of program	Location	Source of information	Basic monthly cost
1	Boarding school	Georgia	Referral service	$3,166
2	Boot camp	Missouri	Referral service	4,500
3	Boarding school	North Carolina	Referral service	4,500
4	Boarding school	South Carolina	Referral service	3,166
5	Boarding school	South Carolina	Referral service	2,795
6	Boarding school	Colorado	Program	2,795 - 2,995
7	Boarding school	Georgia	Program	8,120[a]
8	Boarding school	Montana	Program	3,495
9	Boarding school	New York	Program	5,160
10	Boarding school	Tennessee	Program	8,700[b]
11	Boarding school	Utah	Program	6,500[b]
12	Wilderness program	Georgia	Program	12,600
13	Wilderness program	North Carolina	Program	13,020
14	Wilderness program	Texas	Program	13,020

Source: GAO analysis of information obtained during undercover calls to programs and referral services.

[a] This is for the first 90 days; the cost drops afterwards.

[b] This includes therapy.

End Notes

[1] GAO, *Residential Treatment Programs: Concerns Regarding Abuse and Death in Certain Programs for Troubled Youth*, GAO-08-146T (Washington, D.C.: Oct. 10, 2007).

[2] 42 C.F.R. §§ 483.350 - .376.

[3] For an illustration showing the states where victims resided and the location of the programs they attended, both for this testimony and our October 2007 testimony, see app. I.

In: When Abuse and Neglect Occur at Residential… ISBN: 978-1-60876-965-0
Editor: Kirsten S. Madsen pp.53-88

Chapter 3

RESIDENTIAL TREATMENT PROGRAMS: CONCERNS REGARDING ABUSE AND DEATH IN CERTAIN PROGRAMS FOR TROUBLED YOUTH*

Gregory D. Kutz and Andy O'Connell

WHY GAO DID THIS STUDY

Residential treatment programs provide a range of services, including drug and alcohol treatment, confidence building, military-style discipline, and psychological counseling for troubled boys and girls with a variety of addiction, behavioral, and emotional problems. This testimony concerns programs across the country referring to themselves as wilderness therapy programs, boot camps, and academies, among other names.

Many cite positive outcomes associated with specific types of residential treatment. There are also allegations regarding the abuse and death of youth enrolled in residential treatment programs. Given concerns about these allegations, particularly in reference to private programs, the Committee asked GAO to (1) verify whether allegations of abuse and death at residential

---

* This is an edited, reformatted and augmented version of a U. S. Government Accountability Office publication dated October 2007.

treatment prog* This is an edited, reformatted and augmented version of a U. S. Government Accountability Office publication dated October 2007.rams are widespread and (2) examine the facts and circumstances surrounding selected closed cases where a teenager died while enrolled in a private program.

To achieve these objectives, GAO conducted numerous interviews and examined documents from closed cases dating as far back as 1990, including police reports, autopsy reports, and state agency oversight reviews and investigations. GAO did not attempt to evaluate the benefits of residential treatment programs or verify the facts regarding the thousands of allegations it reviewed.

What GAO Found

GAO found thousands of allegations of abuse, some of which involved death, at residential treatment programs across the country and in American-owned and American-operated facilities abroad between the years 1990 and 2007. Allegations included reports of abuse and death recorded by state agencies and the Department of Health and Human Services, allegations detailed in pending civil and criminal trials with hundreds of plaintiffs, and claims of abuse and death that were posted on the Internet. For example, during 2005 alone, 33 states reported 1,619 staff members involved in incidents of abuse in residential programs. GAO could not identify a more concrete number of allegations because it could not locate a single Web site, federal agency, or other entity that collects comprehensive nationwide data.

GAO also examined, in greater detail, 10 closed civil or criminal cases from 1990 through 2004 where a teenager died while enrolled in a private program. GAO found significant evidence of ineffective management in most of the 10 cases, with program leaders neglecting the needs of program participants and staff. This ineffective management compounded the negative consequences of (and sometimes directly resulted in) the hiring of untrained staff; a lack of adequate nourishment; and reckless or negligent operating practices, including a lack of adequate equipment. These factors played a significant role in the deaths GAO examined. See the table below for detailed information related to three of the case studies.

Examples of Case Studies GAO Examined

Sex/age	Date of death	Cause of death	Case details
Female, 15	May 1990	Dehydration	• Showed signs of illness for 2 days, such as blurred vision, vomiting water, and frequent stumbling • Program staff thought she was faking her illness to get out of the program • Collapsed and died while hiking • Lay dead in the road for 18 hours • Program brochure advertised staff as "highly trained survival experts"
Male, 15	Sept. 2000	Internal bleeding	• Head-injury victim with behavioral challenges who refused to return to campsite • Restrained by staff and held face down in the dirt for 45 minutes • Died of a severed artery in the neck • Death ruled a homicide
Male, 14	July 2002	Hyper-thermia (high body temperature)	• Experienced difficulty while hiking and sat down, breathing heavily and moaning • Fainted and lay motionless • One staff member hid behind a tree for 10 minutes to see whether the victim was "faking it" • Staff member returned and found no pulse • Died soon afterwards

Source: Records including police reports, legal documents, and state investigative documents.

Mr. Chairman and Members of the Committee:

Thank you for the opportunity to discuss residential treatment programs for troubled youth. In the context of this testimony, we are using the term residential treatment program to refer to entities across the country and abroad calling themselves wilderness therapy programs, boarding schools, academies, behavioral modification facilities, and boot camps, among other names. While some of these programs are funded publicly by state and local government agencies, others are privately owned and operated. Private residential treatment programs typically market their services to the parents of troubled teenagers—boys and girls with a variety of addiction, behavioral, and emotional problems—and provide a range of services, including drug and alcohol treatment, confidence building, military-style discipline, and psychological counseling for illnesses such as depression and attention deficit disorder.

Many cite positive outcomes associated with specific types of residential treatment. There are also allegations regarding the abuse and death of youth enrolled in residential treatment programs. Given concerns about these allegations, particularly in reference to private programs, you asked us to (1) verify whether allegations of abuse and death at residential treatment programs are widespread and (2) examine the facts and circumstances surrounding selected closed cases where a teenager died while enrolled in a private program.

To verify whether allegations of abuse and death at residential treatment programs are widespread, we gathered available information about allegations made over the last 17 years by performing interviews with relevant experts, reviewing relevant studies and documents, conducting Internet searches for Web sites making allegations, reviewing data from the National Child Abuse and Neglect Data System (NCANDS),[1] and reviewing relevant state and federal court documents. We were unable to disaggregate information on public and private programs; consequently, the information we present includes allegations against both types.

To select our case studies, we identified numerous closed civil and criminal cases in which a court was asked to decide whether a private residential treatment program was responsible for the death of an enrolled teenager. When identifying our cases, we specifically excluded teenager deaths at public programs such as state-sponsored foster programs, juvenile justice programs for delinquent youth, or programs that exclusively treat psychological disorders or substance abuse in a hospital setting. We focused on deaths between the years 1990 and 2004 to illustrate the long-standing issues presented by private residential treatment programs. We limited our cases to closed cases and, thus, ongoing cases from the last several years were not included in our work. We selected these 10 cases based on several factors including victim age, program location, type of program the victim attended, and date of death.

We then examined, in more detail, the facts and circumstances of the death and any related abuse of the victim. To validate the facts and circumstances of each case, and to the extent possible, we conducted interviews with related parties, including current and former program staff and officials, attorneys and law enforcement officials involved in the cases, and the parents of the victims. Further, we reviewed available documentation to support the facts of each case including (but not limited to) marketing materials, police reports, autopsy reports, and state agency oversight reviews and investigations. In addition, we conducted site visits at nine residential treatment programs to obtain a firsthand perspective on how residential treatment programs operate. Five of these nine programs were related to the still-operational programs discussed in our cases— either because they were the same program or represented a permutation of the original program operating under a different name or in a new location. Where we obtained financial information about the programs, we converted this information to 2007 dollars so that the information was comparable.

It is important to emphasize that residential treatment programs are intended to help youth with serious problems—in some cases, these problems constitute life-threatening addictions and diseases. We did not attempt to evaluate the benefits of residential treatment programs in dealing with these serious problems. Moreover, it is not possible to generalize the results of our investigation as applying to all residential treatment programs, whether privately or publicly funded. We found it difficult to obtain an overall picture of the extent of the residential treatment program industry. For example, while states often regulate publicly funded programs, a number of states do not license or otherwise regulate private programs. Because programs determine how to describe themselves, especially in their marketing materials, there is no standard definition for "wilderness therapy program," "boot camp," or other terms used to describe the types of programs and facilities considered to be part of this industry. GAO is completing a comprehensive review of state and federal oversight of residential treatment programs for youth with behavioral and emotional challenges and expects to report next year.

We performed our work from June through September of 2007 in accordance with the quality standards for investigations set forth by the President's Council on Integrity and Efficiency.

SUMMARY

We found thousands of allegations of abuse, some of which involved death, at residential treatment programs across the country and in American-owned and American-operated facilities abroad between the years 1990 and 2007. Allegations included reports of abuse and death recorded by state agencies and the Department of Health and Human Services, allegations detailed in pending civil and criminal cases with hundreds of plaintiffs, and claims of abuse and death that were posted on the Internet. For example, according to the most recent NCANDS data, during 2005 alone 33 states reported 1,619 staff members involved in incidents of abuse in residential programs. Because there are no specific reporting requirements or definitions for private programs in particular, we could not determine what percentage of the thousands of allegations we found are related to such programs.

We also examined, in greater detail, 10 closed cases where a teenager died while enrolled in a private program. We found significant evidence of ineffective management in most of these 10 cases, with program leaders neglecting the needs of program participants and staff. This ineffective management compounded the negative consequences of (and sometimes directly resulted in) the hiring of untrained staff; a lack of adequate nourishment; and reckless or negligent operating practices, including a lack of adequate equipment. These factors played a significant role in most of the deaths we examined. For example:

- In May 1990, a 15-year-old female was enrolled in a 9-week wilderness program. Although the program brochure claimed that counselors were "highly trained survival experts," they did not recognize the signs of dehydration when she began complaining of blurred vision, stumbling, and vomiting water 3 days into a hike. According to police documents, on the fifth day and after nearly 2 days of serious symptoms, the dying teen finally collapsed and became unresponsive, at which point counselors attempted to signal for help using a fire because they were not equipped with radios. Police documents state that the victim lay dead in a dirt road for 18 hours before rescuers arrived.
- In another example, we learned that, in July 2001, a 14-year-old male enrolled in a boot camp became so dehydrated that he began to eat dirt from the desert floor. Witnesses said that when he eventually fell unconscious and appeared to have a seizure, the program director told staff members to put the victim in the flatbed of a pickup truck and drive him to a hotel. When they could not revive him at the hotel, they put him back in the flatbed of the truck, returned to the camp, and placed the teen's limp body onto his sleeping bag. The program director assured his staff that "everything will be okay" but the victim died soon afterwards.
- In December 2001, on Christmas Day, a 16-year-old female was climbing in an extremely dangerous area unsupervised by program staff. According to documents we reviewed, the girl slipped, fell about 50 feet into a crevasse, and died of massive brain trauma about 3 weeks later. An investigation revealed numerous licensing and safety violations with the program, including an improperly low staff-to-

youth ratio, failure of staff to scout the hiking location prior to the hike, and no first aid kit (it was left at the base camp).

BACKGROUND

Since the early 1990s, hundreds of residential treatment programs and facilities have been established in the United States by state agencies and private companies. Many of these programs are intended to provide a less-restrictive alternative to incarceration or hospitalization for youth who may require intervention to address emotional or behavioral challenges. As mentioned earlier, it is difficult to obtain an overall picture of the extent of this industry. According to a 2006 report by the Substance Abuse and Mental Health Services Administration, state officials identified 71 different types of residential treatment programs for youth with mental illness across the country.[2] A wide range of government or private entities, including government agencies and faith-based organizations, can operate these programs. Each residential treatment program may focus on a specific client type, such as those with substance abuse disorders or suicidal tendencies. In addition, the programs provide a range of services, either on-site or through links with community programs, including educational, medical, psychiatric, and clinical/mental health services.

Regarding oversight of residential treatment programs, states have taken a variety of approaches ranging from statutory regulations that require licensing to no oversight. States differ in how they license and monitor the various types of programs in terms of both the agencies involved and the types of requirements. For example, some states have centralized licensing and monitoring within a single agency, while other states have decentralized these functions among three or more different agencies. There are currently no federal laws that define and regulate residential treatment programs. However, three federal agencies—the Departments of Health and Human Services, Justice, and Education—administer programs that can provide funds to states to support eligible youth who have been placed in some residential treatment programs. For example, the Department of Health and Human Services, through its Administration for Children and Families, administers programs that provide funding to states for a wide range of child welfare services, including foster care, as well as improved handling, investigation, and prosecution of youth maltreatment cases.[3]

In addition to the lack of a standard, commonly recognized definition for residential treatment programs, there are no standard definitions for specific types of programs—wilderness therapy programs, boot camps, and boarding schools, for instance. For our purposes, we define these programs based on the characteristics we identified during our review of the 10 case studies. For example, in the context of our report, we defined wilderness therapy program to mean a program that places youth in different natural environments, including forests, mountains, and deserts. Figure 1 shows images we took near the wilderness therapy programs we visited.

According to wilderness therapy program material, these settings are intended to remove the "distractions" and "temptations" of modern life from teens, forcing them to focus on themselves and their relationships. Included as part of a wilderness training program, participants keep journals that often include entries related to why they are in the program and their experiences and goals while in the wilderness. These journals, which program staff read, are part of the individual and group therapy provided in the field. As part of the wilderness experience, these programs also teach basic survival skills, such as setting up a tent and camp, starting a fire, and cooking food. Figure 2 is photo montage of living arrangements for youth enrolled in the wilderness programs we visited.

Source: GAO.

Note: These images show the surroundings that youth enrolled in a wilderness treatment program might encounter. Clockwise from the upper left, these images show (1) West Virginia woodlands, (2) an Oregon river, and (3) a Utah mountain range.

Figure 1. Environments Where Wilderness Therapy Programs Operate

Source: GAO.

Note: The top two images show living arrangements at two wilderness therapy programs—a "time out" shelter (upper left) and an enrolled youth's campsite (upper right). The bottom two images show the girls' tent (lower left) and the shelter for group therapy and meetings (lower right) for the middle phase of a residential treatment program.

Figure 2. Living Arrangements at Wilderness Therapy Programs GAO Visited

Source: GAO.

Note: These images show the interior of a boot camp facility. Clockwise from the upper left, the images show (1) the overall layout of "the boot camp" room in the facility, where male enrollees spend the majority of their indoor time and sleep on the floor; (2) the limited supplies and personal items of enrollees, including a rolled sleeping bag and mat; (3) bathroom facilities; and (4) a room with bunk beds for youth in the advanced phase of the program.

Figure 3. Interior of a Boot Camp Facility That GAO Visited

Some wilderness therapy programs may include a boot camp element. However, many boot camps (which can also be called behavioral modification facilities) exist independently of wilderness training. In the context of our report, a boot camp is a residential treatment program in which strict discipline and regime are dominant principles. Some military- style boot camp programs also emphasize uniformity and austere living conditions. Figure 3 is a photo montage illustrating a boot camp which minimizes creature comfort and emphasizes organization and discipline.

A third type of residential treatment program is known as a boarding school. Although these programs may combine wilderness or boot camp elements, boarding schools (also called academies) are generally advertised as providing academic education beyond the survival skills a wilderness therapy program might teach. This academic education is sometimes approved by the state in which the program operates and may also be transferable as elective credits toward high school. These programs often enroll youth whose parents force them to attend against their will. The schools can include fences and other security measures to ensure that youth do not leave without permission. Figure 4 shows some of the features boarding schools may employ to keep youth in the facilities.

A variety of ancillary services related to residential treatment programs are available for an additional fee in some programs. These services include:

- Referral services and educational consultants to assist parents in selecting a program.
- Transport services to pick up a youth and bring him or her to the program. Parents frequently use a transport service if their child is unwilling to attend the program.
- Additional individual, group, or family counseling or therapy sessions as part of treatment. These services may be located on the premises or nearby.
- Financial services, such as loans, to assist parents in covering the expense of residential treatment programs.

These services are marketed toward parents and, with the exception of financial services, are not regulated by the federal government.

Source: GAO.

Note: These images show the exterior of a boarding school. Clockwise from the upper left, the images show (1) a close-up of the video surveillance equipment and motion detectors in place on the outside of the school; (2) tall exterior fencing and motion detector; and (3) an angle of the facility exterior that clearly displays security features, including video monitoring, lighting, fencing, and wire mesh over the windows.

Figure 4. Security Features Employed at a Boarding School GAO Visited

WIDESPREAD ALLEGATIONS OF ABUSE AND DEATH AT RESIDENTIAL TREATMENT PROGRAMS

We found thousands of allegations of abuse, some of which involved death, at public and private residential treatment programs across the country between the years 1990 and 2007. We are unable to identify a more concrete number of allegations because we could not locate a single Web site, federal agency, or other entity that collects comprehensive nationwide data related to this issue. Although the NCANDS database, operated by the Department of Health and Human Services, collects some data from states, data submission is voluntary and not all states with residential treatment programs contribute information. According to the most recent NCANDS data, during 2005 alone 33 states reported 1,619 staff members involved in incidents of abuse in residential programs. Because of limited data collection and reporting, we could not determine the numbers of incidents of abuse and death associated with private programs.

It is important to emphasize that allegations should not be confused with proof of actual abuse. However, in terms of meeting our objective, the thousands of allegations we found came from a number of sources besides NCANDS. For example:

- We identified claims of abuse and death in pending and closed civil or criminal proceedings with dozens of plaintiffs alleging abuse. For instance, according to one pending civil lawsuit filed as recently as July 2007, dozens of parents allege that their children were subjected to over 30 separate types of abuse.
- We found attorneys around the country who represent youth and groups of youth who allege that abuse took place while these youth were enrolled in residential treatment programs. For example, an attorney based in New Jersey with whom we spoke has counseled dozens of youth who alleged they were abused in residential treatment programs in past cases, as has another attorney, a retired prosecutor, who advocates for abuse victims.
- We found that allegations are posted on various Web sites advocating for the shutdown of certain programs. Past participants in wilderness programs and other youth residential treatment programs have individually or collectively set up sites claiming abuse and death. The Internet contains an unknown number of such Web sites. One site on the Internet, for example, identifies over 100 youth who it claims died in various programs. In other instances, parents of victims who have died or were abused in these programs have similarly set up an unknown number of Web sites. Conversely, there are also an unknown number of sites that promote and advocate the benefits of various programs.

Because there are no specific reporting requirements or definitions for private programs in particular, we could not determine what percentage of the thousands of allegations we found are related to such programs. There is likely a small percentage of overlapping allegations given our inability to reconcile information from the sources we used.

CASES OF DEATH AT SELECTED RESIDENTIAL TREATMENT PROGRAMS

We selected 10 closed cases from private programs to examine in greater detail. Specifically, these cases were focused on the death of a teenager in a private residential treatment program that occurred between 1990 and 2004. We found significant evidence of ineffective management in most of these 10 cases, with many examples of how program leaders neglected the needs of program participants and staff. In some cases, program leaders gave their staff bad advice when they were alerted to the health problems of a teen. In other cases, program leaders appeared to be so concerned with boosting enrollment that they told parents their programs could provide services that they were not qualified to offer and could not provide. Several cases reveal program leaders who claimed to have credentials in therapy or medicine that they did not have, leading parents to trust them with teens who had serious mental or physical disabilities requiring proper treatment. These ineffective management techniques compounded the negative consequences of (and sometimes directly resulted in) the hiring of untrained staff; a lack of adequate nourishment; and reckless or negligent operating practices, including a lack of adequate equipment. These specific factors played a significant role in most of the deaths we examined.

- **Untrained staff.** A common theme of many of the cases we examined is that staff misinterpreted legitimate medical emergencies. Rather than recognizing the signs of dehydration, heat stroke, or illness, staff assumed that a dying teen was in fact attempting to use trickery to get out of the program. This resulted in the death of teenagers from common, treatable illnesses. In some cases, teens who fell ill from less- common ailments exhibited their symptoms for many days, dying slowly while untrained staff continued to believe the teen was "faking it." Unfortunately, in almost all of our cases, staff only realized that a teen was in distress when it was already too late.

- **Lack of adequate nourishment.** In many cases, program philosophy (e.g., "tough love") was taken to such an extreme that teenagers were undernourished. One program fed teenagers an apple for breakfast, a carrot for lunch, and a bowl of beans for dinner while requiring extensive physical activity in harsh conditions. Another program forced teenagers to fast for 2 days. Teenagers were also given equal rations of food regardless of their height, weight, or other dietary needs. In this program, an ill teenager lost 20 percent of his body weight over the course of about a month. Unbeknownst to staff, the teenager was simultaneously suffering from a perforated ulcer.

- **Reckless or negligent operating practices.** In at least two cases, program staff set out to lead hikes in unfamiliar territory that they had not scouted in advance. Important items such as radios and first aid kits were left behind. In another case, program operators did not take into account the need for an adjustment period between a teenager's comfortable home life and the wilderness; this endangered the safety of one teenager, who suddenly found herself in an unfamiliar environment. State licensing initiatives attempt, in part, to minimize the risk that some programs may endanger teenagers through reckless and negligent practices; however, not all programs we examined were covered by operating licenses. Furthermore, some licensed programs deviated from the terms of their licenses, leading states, after the death of a teen, to take action against programs that had flouted health and safety guidelines.

See table 1 for a summary of the cases we examined.

Case One

The victim was a 15-year-old female. Her parents told us that she was a date-rape victim who suffered from depression, and that in 1990 she enrolled in a 9-week wilderness program in Utah to build confidence and improve her self-esteem. The victim and her parents found out about the program through a friend who claimed to know the owner. The parents of the victim spoke with the owner of the program several times and reviewed brochures from the owner. The brochure stated that the program's counselors were "highly trained survival experts" and that "the professional experience and expertise" of its staff was "unparalleled." The fees and tuition for the program cost a little over $20,600 (or about $327 per day). The victim and her parents ultimately decided that this program would meet their needs and pursued enrollment.

Table 1. Summary of Victim Information

Case	Victim information	Program attended	Date of death	Cause of death	Case details
1	Female, 15, California resident	Utah wilderness therapy program (death occurred in Arizona)	May 1990	Dehydration	Died while hiking on fifth day of program Exhibited signs of illness for 2 days, such as throwing up water, falling down, and complaining of blurred vision Collapsed due to dehydration Lay dead for 18 hours on dirt road Program brochure given to parents had advertised program staff as "highly trained survival experts" Died on federal land
2	Female, 16, Florida resident	Utah wilderness therapy program	June 1990	Heat stroke	Died while hiking on third day of program Program had not considered child's adjustment from a coastal, sea-level residence to a high desert wilderness area Died of "exertional heatstroke" while hiking Program owner acquitted of criminal charges but placed on state list of suspected child abusers
3	Male, 16, Arizona resident	Utah wilderness therapy program	March 1994	Acute infection resulting from perforated ulcer	Exhibited signs of physical distress for nearly 3 weeks, such as severe abdominal pain, significant weight loss (20 percent of body weight), loss of bodily functions, and weakness Collapsed and became unresponsive Air lifted to hospital and pronounced dead on arrival Died on federal land

Table 1. (Contined)

Case	Victim information	Program attended	Date of death	Cause of death	Case details
4	Male, 15, Oregon resident	Oregon wilderness therapy program	Sept. 2000	Severed artery	Refused to return to campsite but did not behave violently Restrained by staff and held face down to the ground for almost 45 minutes Died of severed artery in neck Death ruled a homicide Grand jury declined to issue an indictment Died on federal land
5	Male, 14, Massa-chusetts resident	West Virginia residential school and wilderness therapy program	Feb. 2001	Suicide (hanging)	Attempted suicide twice before enrolling in program On the fifth day of program cut arm several times with camp-issued pocket knife Staff did not take the knife away Hung himself near his tent the next day Program had no suicide prevention plan
6	Male, 14, Arizona resident	Arizona boot camp	July 2001	Dehydration	On seventh day was punished for asking to go home Forced to sit in 113-degree desert heat Was delirious and dehydrated Taken to motel room, placed in shower tub, left unattended Staff returned victim to camp in the flatbed of a pickup truck and placed his limp body onto his sleeping bag Staff later found him unresponsive and he died at the hospital

Table 1. (Continued)

Case	Victim information	Program attended	Date of death	Cause of death	Case details
7	Female, 16, Virginia resident	Utah wilde-rness therapy program	Jan. 2002	Massive head trauma	Fell while hiking on Christmas Day Staff had not scouted extremely dangerous area beforehand Staff had no medical equipment, against its licensing agreement Took about one hour for first paramedics to arrive Died on federal land
8	Female, 15, California resident	Oregon wilderness therapy program (also operated in Nevada at time of death)	May 2002	Dehydration / heat stroke	Died while hiking on first day of program Told others she had taken methamphetamines before the hike, but Was not screened for drug before hike Experienced signs of distress for several hours while hiking Collapsed and stopped breathing Died of heat stroke complicated by the methamphetamines and prescription medication Died on federal land
9	Male, 14, Texas resident	Utah wilderness therapy program	July 2002	Hyper-thermia (excessive body temperature)	On a 3-mile hike in desert heat Complained of thirst and refused to continue hike Left in the sun for an hour and stopped breathing Staff member hid behind a tree for 10 minutes thinking the victim was "faking" illness Help arrived over an hour after death Died on federal land

Table 1. (Continued)

Case	Victim information	Program attended	Date of death	Cause of death	Case details
10	Male, 15, California resident	Missouri boot camp and boarding school	Nov. 2004	Compli-cations of Rhabdomyo-lysis due to a probable spider bite	Displayed signs of distress for several days Program's medical officer told staff victim was “faking it” Became lifeless and could hardly move Punished for being too weak to exercise and forced to wear a 20-pound sandbag around his neck Autopsy reported death was caused by complications of habdomyolysis due to a probable spider bite, but also found umerous bruises all over the victim's body

Source: Records including police reports, legal documents, and state investigative documents.

The victim's parents said they trusted the brochures, the program owner, and the program staff. However, the parents were not informed that the program was completely new and that their daughter would be going on the program's first wilderness trek. Program staff were not familiar with the area, relied upon maps and a compass to navigate the difficult terrain, and became lost. As a result, they crossed into the state of Arizona and wandered onto Bureau of Land Management (BLM) land. According to a lawsuit filed by her parents, the victim complained of general nausea, was not eating, and began vomiting water on about the third day of the 5-day hike. Staff ignored her complaints and thought she was "faking it" to get out of the program. Police documents indicate that the two staff members leading the hike stated that they did not realize the victim was slowly dehydrating, despite the fact that she was vomiting water and had not eaten any food.

On the fifth day of the hike, the victim fell several times and was described by the other hikers as being "in distress." It does not appear that staff took any action to help her. At about 5:45 p.m. on the fifth day, the victim collapsed in the road and stopped breathing. According to police records, staff did not call for help because they were not equipped with radios— instead, they performed CPR and attempted to signal for help using a signal fire. CPR did not revive the victim; she died by the side of the road and her body was covered with a tarp. The following afternoon, a BLM helicopter airlifted her body to a nearby city for autopsy. The death certificate for the victim states that she died of dehydration due to exposure. Although local police investigated the death, no charges were filed. Utah officials wanted to pursue the case, but they did not have grounds to do so because the victim died in Arizona. The parents of the victim filed a civil suit and settled out of court for an undisclosed sum.

Soon after the victim's death and 6 months after opening, the founder closed the program and moved to Nevada, where she operated in that state until her program was ordered to close by authorities there. In a hearing granting a preliminary judgment that enjoined the operator of the program, the judge said that he would not shelter this program, which was in effect hiding from the controls of the adjoining state. He chastised the program owner for running a money-making operation while trying to escape the oversight of the state, writing, "[The owner] wishes to conduct a wilderness survival program for children for profit, without state regulation" and she "hide[s] the children from the investigating state authorities and appear[s] uncooperative towards them." He expressed further concerns, including a statement that participants in the program did not appear to be receiving "adequate care and protection" and that qualified and competent counselors were not in charge of the program. The judge also noted that one of the adult counselors was "an ex-felon and a fugitive." After this program closed, the program founder returned to Utah and joined yet another program where another death occurred 5 years later (this death is detailed in case seven). We found that the founder of this residential treatment program had a history in the industry—prior to opening the program discussed in this case, she worked as an administrator in the program covered in another case (case two). Today, the program founder is still working in the industry as a consultant, providing advice to parents who may not know of her history.

Case Two

The victim was a 16-year-old female who had just celebrated her birthday. According to her mother, in 1990 the victim was enrolled in a 9-week wilderness therapy program because she suffered from depression and struggled with drug abuse. The victim's mother obtained brochures from the program owner and discussed the program with him and other program staff. According to the mother, the program owner answered all her questions and "really sold the program." She told us:

> "I understood there would be highly trained and qualified people with [my daughter] who could handle any emergency... they boasted of a 13-year flawless safety record, [and] I thought to myself 'why should I worry? Why would anything happen to her?'"

Believing that the program would help her daughter, the victim's mother and stepfather secured a personal loan to pay the $25,600 in tuition for the program (or about $400 per day). She also paid about $4,415 to have a transport service come to the family home and take her daughter to the program. The victim's mother and stepfather hired the service because they were afraid their daughter would run away when told that she was being enrolled in the program. According to the victim's mother, two people came to the family home at 4 a.m. to take her daughter to the program's location in the Utah desert, where a group hike was already under way.

Three days into the program, the victim collapsed and died while hiking. According to the program brochure, the first 5 days of the program are "days and nights of physical and mental stress with forced march, night hikes, and limited food and water. Youth are stripped mentally and physically of material facades and all manipulatory tools." After the victim collapsed, one of the counselors on the hike administered CPR until an emergency helicopter and nurse arrived to take the victim to a hospital, where she was pronounced dead. According to the victim's mother, her daughter died of "exertional heatstroke." The program had not made any accommodation or allowed for any adjustment for the fact that her daughter had traveled from a coastal, sea-level residence in Florida to the high desert wilderness of Utah. The mother of the victim also said that program staff did not have salt tablets or other supplies that are commonly used to offset the affects of heat.

Shortly after the victim died, the 9-week wilderness program closed. A state hearing brought to light complaints of child abuse in the program and the owner of the program was charged with negligent homicide. He was acquitted of criminal charges. However, the state child protective services agency concluded that child abuse had occurred and placed the owner on Utah's registry of child abusers, preventing him from working in the state at a licensed child treatment facility. Two other program staff agreed to cooperate with the prosecution to avoid standing trial; these staff were given probation and prohibited from being involved with similar programs for up to 5 years. In 1994, the divorced parents of the victim split a $260,000 settlement resulting from a civil suit against the owner.

After this program closed, its owner opened and operated a number of domestic and foreign residential treatment programs over the next several years. Although he was listed on the Utah registry of suspected child abusers, the program owner opened and operated these programs elsewhere—many of which were ultimately shut down by state officials and foreign governments because of alleged and proven child abuse. At least one of these programs is still operating abroad and is marketed on the Internet, along with 10 other programs considered to be part of the same network. As discussed above, the program owner in our first case originally worked in this program as an administrator before it closed.

Case Three

The victim was a 16-year-old male. According to his parents, in 1994 they enrolled him in a 9-week wilderness therapy program in Utah because of minor drug use, academic underachievement, and association with a new peer group that was having a negative impact on him. The parents learned of the program from an acquaintance and got a program brochure that "looked great" in their opinion. They thought the program was well-suited for their son because it was an outdoor program focusing on small groups of youth who were about the same age. They spoke with the program owner and his wife, who flew to Phoenix, Arizona, to talk with them. To be able to afford the program's cost of about $18,500 (or $263 per day), the victim's parents told us they took out a second mortgage on their house. They also paid nearly $2,000 to have their son transported to the campsite in the program owner's private plane. At the time they enrolled their son, the parents were unaware that this program was started by two former employees of a program where a teenager had died (this program is discussed in our second case).

According to the victim's father, his son became sick around the 11th day of the program. According to court and other documents, the victim began exhibiting signs of physical distress and suffered from severe abdominal pain, weakness, weight loss, and loss of bodily functions. Although the victim collapsed several times during daily hikes, accounts we reviewed indicate that staff ignored the victim's pleas for help. He was forced to continue on for 20 days in this condition. After his final collapse 31 days into the program, staff could not detect any respiration or pulse. Only at this time did staff radio program headquarters and request help, although they were expected to report any illnesses or disciplinary incidents and had signed an agreement when employed stating that they were responsible for "the safety and welfare of fellow staff members and students." The victim was airlifted to a nearby hospital and was pronounced dead upon arrival. The 5-foot 10-inch victim, already a thin boy, had dropped from 131 to 108 pounds—a loss of nearly 20 percent of his body weight during his month-long enrollment.[4]

The victim's father told us that when he was notified of his son's death, he could only think that "some terrible accident" had occurred. But according to the autopsy report, the victim died of acute peritonitis—an infection related to a perforated ulcer. This condition would have been treatable provided there had been early medical attention. The father told us that the mortician, against his usual policy, showed him the condition of his son's body because it was "something that needed to be investigated." The victim's father told us he "buckled at the knees" when he saw the body of his son—emaciated and covered with cuts, bruises, abrasions, blisters, and a full-body rash; what he saw was unrecognizable as his son except for a childhood scar above the eye.

In the wake of the death, the state revoked the program's operating license. According to the state's licensing director, the program closed 3 months later because the attorney general's office had initiated an investigation into child abuse in the program, although no abuse was found after examining the 30 to 40 youth who were also enrolled in the program when the victim died. The state attorney general's office and a local county prosecutor filed criminal charges against the program owners and several staff members. After a change of venue, one defendant went to trial and was convicted of "abuse or neglect of a disabled child" in this case. Five other defendants pleaded guilty to a number of other charges— five guilty pleas on negligent homicide and two on failure to comply with a license. The defendants in the case were sentenced to probation and community service. The parents of the victim subsequently filed a civil suit that was settled out of court for an undisclosed amount.

Case Four

The victim was a 15-year-old male. According to the victim's mother, in 2000 she enrolled her son in a wilderness program in Oregon to build his confidence and develop self-esteem in the wake of a childhood car accident. The accident had resulted in her son sustaining a severe head injury, among other injuries. After an extensive Internet search and discussions with representatives of various wilderness programs and camps for head-injury victims, the mother told us she selected a program that she believed would meet her son's needs. What "sold me on the program," she said, was the program owner's repeated assurances over the telephone that the program was "a perfect fit" for her son. She told us that to pay for the $27,500 program, she withdrew money from her retirement account. The program was between 60 to 90 days (about $305 to $450 per day) depending on a youth's progression through the program.

The victim's mother said that she became suspicious about the program when she dropped her son off. She said that the program director and another staff person disregarded her statements about her son's "likes and dislikes," despite believing that the program would take into account the personal needs of her son. Later, she filed a lawsuit alleging that the staff had no experience dealing with brain-injured children and others with certain handicaps who were in the program. What she also did not know was that the founder of the program was himself a former employee of two other wilderness programs in another state where deaths had occurred (we discuss these programs in cases two and three). The program founder also employed staff who had been charged with child abuse while employed at other wilderness programs.

According to her lawsuit, her son left the program headquarters on a group hike with three counselors and three other students. Several days into the multiday hike, while camping under permit on BLM land, the victim refused to return to the campsite after being escorted by a counselor about 200 yards to relieve himself. Two counselors then attempted to lead him back to the campsite. According to an account of the incident, when he continued to refuse, they tried to force him to return and they all fell to the ground together. The two counselors subsequently held the victim face down in the dirt until he stopped struggling; by one account a counselor sat on the victim for almost 45 minutes. When the counselors realized the victim was no longer breathing, they telephoned for help and requested a 9-1-1 operator's advice on administering CPR. The victim's mother told us that she found out about the situation when program staff called to tell her that her son was being airlifted to a medical center. Shortly afterwards, a nurse called and urged her to come to the hospital with her husband. They were not able to make it in time—on the drive to the hospital, her son's doctor called, advised her to pull to the side of the road, and informed her that her son had died. The victim's mother told us that she was informed, after the autopsy, that the main artery in her son's neck had been torn. The cause of death was listed as a homicide.

In September 2000, after the boy's death, one of the counselors was charged with criminally negligent homicide. A grand jury subsequently declined to indict him. The victim's mother told us that at the grand jury hearing, she found out from parents of other youth in the program that they had been charged different amounts of money for the same program, and that program officials had told them what they wanted to hear about the program's ability to meet each of their children's special needs. In early 2001, the mother of the victim filed a $1.5 million wrongful death lawsuit against the program, its parent company, and its president. The lawsuit was settled in 2002 for an undisclosed amount.

Due in part to the victim's death, in early 2002, Oregon implemented its outdoor licensing requirements. The state's Department of Justice subsequently filed a complaint alleging numerous violations of the state's Unlawful Trade Practices Act and civil racketeering laws, including charges that the program misrepresented its safety procedures and criminally mistreated enrolled youth. In an incident unconnected to this case, the program was also charged with child abuse related to frostbite. As a result of these complaints, in February of 2002, the program entered into agreement with the state's attorney general to modify program operations and pay a $5,000 fee. The program continued to work with the State of Oregon throughout 2002 to comply with the agreement. In the summer of 2002, BLM revoked the camping permit for the program due, in part, to the victim's death. The program closed in December of 2002.

Case Five

The victim was a 14-year-old male. According to his father, in 2001 the victim was enrolled in a private West Virginia residential treatment center and boarding school. He told us that his son had been diagnosed with clinical depression, had attempted suicide twice, was on medication, and was being treated by a psychiatrist. Because their son was having difficulties in his school, the parents—in consultation with their son's psychiatrist—decided their son would benefit by attending a school that was more sensitive to their son's problems. To identify a suitable school, the family hired an education consultant who said he was a member of an educational consultants' association and that he specialized in matching troubled teens with appropriate treatment programs. The parents discussed their son's personality, medical history (including his previous suicide attempts), and treatment needs with the consultant. According to the father, the consultant "quickly" recommended the West Virginia school. The program was licensed by the state and cost almost $23,000 (or about $255 per day).

According to the parents and court documents, the victim committed suicide 6 days into the program. On the day before he killed himself, while participating in the first phase of the program ("survival training"), the victim deliberately cut his left arm four times from wrist to elbow using a pocket knife issued to him by the school. After cutting himself, the victim approached a counselor and showed him what he had done, pleading with the counselor to take the knife away before he hurt himself again.[5] He also asked the counselor to call his mother and tell her that he wanted to go home. The counselor spoke with the victim, elicited a promise from him not to hurt himself again, and gave the knife back. The next evening the victim hung himself with a cord not far from his tent. Four hours passed before the program chose to notify the family about the suicide. When the owner of the program finally called the family to notify them, according to the father, the owner said, "There was nothing we could do."

In the aftermath of the suicide, the family learned that the program did not have any procedures for addressing suicidal behavior even though it had marketed itself as being able to provide appropriate therapy to its students. Moreover, one of the program owners, whom the father considered the head therapist, did not have any formal training to provide therapy. The family also learned that the owner and another counselor had visited their son's campsite, as previously scheduled, the day he died. During this visit, field staff told them about the self-inflicted injury and statements the victim had made the night before. According to the father, the owner then advised field staff that the victim was being manipulative in an attempt to be sent home, and that the staff should ignore him to discourage further manipulative behavior.

The owners and the program were indicted by a grand jury on criminal charges of child neglect resulting in death. According to the transcript, the judge who was assigned to the case pushed the parties not to choose a bench trial to avoid a lengthy and complicated trial. The program owner pleaded no contest to the charge of child neglect resulting in death with a fine of $5,000 in exchange for dismissal of charges. The state conducted an investigation into the circumstances and initially planned to close the program. However, the program owners negotiated an agreement with the state not to shut down the program in exchange for a change of ownership and management. According to the victim's father, the family of the victim subsequently filed a civil suit and a settlement was reached for $1.2 million, which included the owners admitting and accepting personal responsibility for the suicide.

This program remains open and operating. Within the last 18 months, a group of investors purchased the program and are planning to open and operate other programs around the country, according to the program administrators with whom we spoke. As part of our work we also learned that the program has a U.S. Forest Service permit however, because it has not filed all required usage reports nor paid required permit fees in almost 8 years, it is in violation of the terms of the permit. We estimate that the program owes the U.S. Forest Service tens of thousands of dollars, although we could not calculate the actual debt.

Case Six

The victim was a 14-year-old male. According to police documents, the victim's mother enrolled him in a military-style Arizona boot camp in 2001 to address behavioral problems. The mother told us that she "thought it would be a good idea." In addition, she told us that her son suffered from some hearing loss, a learning disability, Attention Deficit Hyperactivity Disorder (ADHD), and depression. To address these issues her son was taking medication and attending therapy sessions. According to the mother, her son's therapist had recommended the program, which he described as a "tough love" program and "what [her son] needed." The mother said she trusted the recommendation of her son's therapist; in addition, she spoke with other parents who had children in the program, who also recommended the program to her. She initially enrolled her son in a daytime Saturday program in the spring of 2001 so he could continue attending regular school during the week. Because her son continued to have behavioral problems, she then enrolled him in the program's 5-week summer camp, which she said cost between $4,600 and $5,700 (between $131 and $162 per day). Her understanding was that strenuous program activities took place in the evening and that during the day youth would be in the shade.

Police documents indicate about 50 youth between the ages of 6 and 17 were enrolled in the summer program. According to police, youth were forced to wear black clothing and to sleep in sleeping bags placed on concrete pads that had been standing in direct sunlight during the day. Both black clothing and concrete absorb heat. Moreover, according to documents subsequently filed by the prosecutor, youth were fed an insufficient diet of a single apple for breakfast, a single carrot for lunch, and a bowl of beans for dinner. On the day the victim died, the temperature was approximately 113 degrees Fahrenheit, according to the investigating detective. His report stated that on that day, the program owner asked whether any youth wanted to leave the program; he then segregated those who wanted to leave the program, which included the victim, and forced them to sit in the midday sun for "several hours" while the other participants were allowed to sit in the shade. Witnesses said that while sitting in the sun, the victim began "eating dirt because he was hungry." Witnesses also stated that the victim "had become delirious and dehydrated... saw water everywhere, and had to 'chase the Indians.'" Later on the victim appeared to have a convulsive seizure, but the camp staff present "felt he was faking," according to the detective's report. One staff member reported that the victim had a pulse rate of 180, more than double what is considered a reasonable resting heart rate for a teenager.[6] The program owner then directed two staff and three youth enrolled in the program to take the victim to the owner's room at a nearby motel to "cool him down and clean up." They placed the victim in the flatbed of a staff member's pickup truck and drove to the motel.

Over the next several hours, the following series of events occurred.

- In the owner's hotel room, the limp victim was stripped and placed into the shower with the water running. The investigating detective told us that the victim was left alone for 15 to 20 minutes for his "privacy." During this time, one of the two staff members telephoned the program owner about the victim's serious condition; the owner is said to have told the staff person that "everything will be okay." However, when staff members returned to the bathroom they saw the victim facedown in the water. The victim had defecated and vomited on himself.
- After cleaning up the victim, a staff member removed him from the shower and placed him on the hotel room floor. Another staff member began pressing the victim's stomach with his hands, at which point, according to the staff member's personal account, mud began oozing out of the victim's mouth. The staff member then used one of his feet to press even harder on the victim's stomach, which resulted in the victim vomiting even more mud and a rock about the size of quarter. At this point, a staff member again called the owner to say the boy was not responding; the owner instructed them to take the victim back to the camp. They placed the victim in the flatbed of the pickup truck for the drive back.
- Staff placed the victim on his sleeping bag upon returning to camp. He was reportedly breathing at this time, but then stopped breathing and was again put in the back of the pickup truck to take him for help. However, one staff member expressed his concern that the boy would die unless they called 9-1-1 immediately. The county sheriff's office reported receiving a telephone call at approximately 9:43 p.m. that evening saying a camp participant "had been eating dirt all day, had refused water, and was now in an unconscious state and not breathing." This is the first recorded instance in which the program owner or staff sought medical attention for the victim. Instructions on how to perform CPR were given and emergency help was dispatched.

The victim was pronounced dead after being airlifted to a local medical center. The medical examiner who conducted the autopsy expressed concern that the victim had not been adequately hydrated and had not received enough food while at the camp. His preliminary ruling on the cause of death was that "of near drowning brought on by dehydration." After a criminal investigation was conducted, the court ultimately concluded that there was "clear and convincing evidence" that program staff were not trained to handle medical emergencies related to dehydration and lack of nutrition. The founder (and chief executive officer) of the program was convicted in 2005 of felony reckless manslaughter and felony aggravated assault and sentenced to 6-year and 5- year terms, respectively. He was also ordered to pay over $7,000 in restitution to the family. In addition, program staff were convicted of various charges, including trespassing, child abuse, and negligent homicide but were put on probation. According to the detective, no staff member at the camp was trained to administer medication or basic medical treatment, including first aid. The mother filed a civil suit that was settled for an undisclosed amount of money. The program closed in 2001.

Case Seven

The victim was a 16-year-old female. Because of defiant, violent behavior, her parents enrolled her in a Utah wilderness and boarding school program in 2001, which was a state-licensed program for youth 13 to 18 years old. The 5 month program cost around $29,000 (or about $193 per day) and operated on both private and federal land. The parents also hired a transport service at a cost of over $3,000 to take their daughter to the program. We found that the director and another executive of this wilderness program had both worked at the same program discussed in our second case and the executive owned the program discussed in our first case.

According to program documents and the statements of staff members, a group hiking in this program would normally require three staff—one in front leading the hike, one in the middle of the group, and one at the end of the group. However, this standard structure had been relaxed on the day the victim fell. It was Christmas Day, and only one staff member accompanied four youth. While hiking in a steep and dangerous area that staff had not previously scouted out, the victim ran ahead of the group with two others, slipped on a steep rock face, and fell more than 50 feet into a crevasse according to statements of the other two youth—one of whom ran back to inform the program staff of the accident. The staff radioed the base camp to report the accident, then called 9-1-1. One of the staff members at the accident scene was an emergency medical technician (EMT) and administered first aid. However, in violation of the program licensing agreement, the first aid kit they were required to have with them had been left at the base camp. An ambulance arrived about 1 hour after the victim fell. First responders decided to have the victim airlifted to a medical center, but the helicopter did not arrive until about 1-1/2 hours after they made the decision to call for an airlift.

According to the coroner's report, the victim died about 3 weeks later in a hospital without ever regaining consciousness. She had suffered massive head trauma, a broken arm, broken teeth, and a collapsed lung. As a result of the death, the state planned to revoke the program's outdoor youth program license based on multiple violations. In addition to an inappropriate staff-to-child ratio (four youth for one staff member, rather than three to one), failure to prescreen the hiking area, and hiking without a first aid kit, the state identified the following additional license violations:

- Program management did not have an emergency or accident plan in place.
- Two of the four staff members who escorted the nine youth in the wilderness had little experience—one had 1 month of program experience and the other had 9 days. Neither of them had completed the required staff training.
- The two most senior staff members on the trip had less than 6 months of wilderness experience—but they remained at the camp while other two inexperienced staff members led the hike.

A lawsuit filed by the family in November 2002 claims that the program did not take reasonable measures to keep the youth in the program safe, especially given the "hiking inexperience" of the youth and the "insufficient number of staff." Specifically, the suit claims that the program's executive director waited for an hour before calling assistance after the victim fell. Additionally, the suit claims that staff only had one radio and no medical equipment or emergency plan. The parents filed an initial lawsuit for $6 million but eventually settled in 2003 for $200,000 before attorneys' fees and health insurance reimbursement were taken out.

The program closed in May 2002 due to fiscal insolvency. However, its parent program—a boarding school licensed by the state—is still in operation. We have not been able to determine whether the wilderness director at the time of the victim's death is still in the industry. However, the other program executive remains in the industry, working as a referral agent for parents seeking assistance in identifying programs for troubled youth.

Case Eight

The victim, who died in 2002, was a 15-year-old female. The parents of the victim told us that she suffered from depression, suicidal thoughts, and bipolar disorder. She also reportedly had a history of drug use, including methamphetamines, marijuana, and cocaine. Her parents explained that they selected a program after researching several programs and consulting with an educational advisor. Although the program was based in Oregon, it operated a 3-week wilderness program in Nevada, which was closer to the family home. The total cost of the program was over $9,200 (or about $438 per day), which included a nonrefundable deposit and over $300 for equipment.

The parents of the victim drove their daughter several hundred miles to enroll her in the program. Because of the distance involved, they stayed overnight in a motel nearby. The next day, when the parents arrived home, they found a phone message waiting for them—it was from the program, saying that their daughter had been in an accident and that she was receiving CPR. According to documents we reviewed, three staff members led seven students on a hike on the first day of the program. The victim fell several times while hiking. The last time she fell, she lost muscle control and had difficulty breathing. The EMT on the expedition had recently completed classroom certification and had no practical field experience. While the staff called for help, the EMT and other staff began CPR and administered epinephrine doses to keep her heart beating during the 3 hours it took a rescue helicopter to arrive. The victim was airlifted to a nearby hospital where she was pronounced dead.

The victim's death was ruled an accident by the coroner—heat stroke complicated by drug-induced dehydration. According to other youth on the hike, they were aware the victim had taken methamphetamines prior to the hike. The victim had had a drug screening done 1 week before entering the program; she tested positive for methamphetamine, which the program director knew but the staff did not. However, the program did not make a determination whether detoxification was necessary, which was required by the state where the program was operating (Nevada), according to a court document. The victim was also taking prescribed psychotropic medications, which affected her body's ability to regulate heat and remain hydrated.

At the time the victim died, this private wilderness treatment program had been in operation for about 15 years in Oregon. Although it claimed to be accredited by the Joint Commission on Heath Care Organizations, this accreditation covered only the base program—not the wilderness program or its drug and alcohol component in which the victim participated.[7] Moreover, even though the wilderness program attended by the victim had been running for 2 years, it was not licensed to operate in Nevada. The district attorney's office declined to file criminal child abuse and neglect charges against two program counselors, although those charges had been recommended by investigating officers. The parents of the victim were never told why criminal charges were never filed. They subsequently filed a civil lawsuit and settled against the program for an undisclosed sum. Two other deaths occurred in this program shortly after the first—one resulted from a previously unknown heart defect and the other from a fallen tree.

Although the wilderness program had a federal permit to operate in Nevada, it was not licensed by that state. After the death, that state investigated and ordered the program closed. The parent company had (and continues to maintain) state licenses in Oregon to operate as a drug and alcohol youth treatment center, an outpatient mental health facility, and an outdoor youth facility, as well as federal land permits from BLM and the U.S. Forest Service. According to program officials, the program has modified its procedures and policies—it no longer enrolls youth taking the medication that affected the victim's ability to regulate her body temperature.

Case Nine

The victim was a 14-year-old male who died in July 2002. According to documents we reviewed, the mother of the victim placed her son in this Utah wilderness program to correct behavioral problems. The victim kept a journal with him during his stay at the program. It stated that he had ADHD and bipolar disorder. His enrollment form indicates that he also had impulse control disorder and that he was taking three prescription medications. His physical examination, performed about 1 month before he entered the program, confirms that he was taking these medications. We could not determine how much the program cost at the time.

According to documents we reviewed, the victim had been in the program for about 8 days when, on a morning hike on BLM land, he began to show signs of hyperthermia (excessively high body temperature). He sat down, breathing heavily and moaning. Two staff members, including one who was an EMT, initially attended to him, but they could not determine if he was truly ill or simply "faking" a problem to get out of hiking. When the victim became unresponsive and appeared to be unconscious, the staff radioed the program director to consult with him. The director advised the staff to move the victim into the shade. The director also suggested checking to see whether the victim was feigning unconsciousness by raising his hand and letting go to see whether it dropped onto his face. They followed the director's instructions. Apparently, because the victim's hand fell to his side rather than his face, the staff member who was an EMT concluded that the victim was only pretending to be ill. While the EMT left to check on other youth in the program, a staff member reportedly hid behind a tree to see whether the victim would get up—reasoning that if the victim were faking sickness, he would get up if he thought nobody was watching. As the victim lay dying, the staff member hid behind the tree for 10 minutes. He failed to see the victim move after this amount of time, so he returned to where the victim lay. He could not find a pulse on the victim. Finally realizing that he was dealing with a medical emergency, the staff member summoned the EMT and they began CPR. The program manager was contacted, and he called for emergency help. Due to difficult terrain and confusion about the exact location of the victim, it took over an hour for the first response team to reach the victim. An attempt to airlift the victim was canceled because a rescue team determined that the victim was already dead.

According to the coroner's report, the victim died of hyperthermia. State Department of Human Services officials initially found no indication that the program had violated its licensing requirements, and the medical examiner could not find any signs of abuse. Subsequently, the Department of Human Services ruled that there were, in fact, licensing violations, and the state charged the program manager and the program owner with child abuse homicide (a second degree felony charge). The program manager was found not guilty of the charges; additionally, it was found that he did not violate the program's license regarding water, nutrition, health care, and other state licensing requirements. Moreover, the court concluded that the State did not prove that the program owner engaged in reckless behavior. Later that year, however, an administrative law judge affirmed the Department of Human Services' decision to revoke the program's license after the judge found that there was evidence of violations. The owner complied with the judge and closed the program in late 2003. About 16 months later, the owner applied for and received a new license to start a new program. According to the Utah director of licensing, as of September 2007, there have been "no problems" with the new program. We could not find conclusive information as to whether the parents of the victim filed a civil case and, if so, what the outcome was.

Case Ten

The victim was a 15-year-old male. According to investigative reports compiled after his death, the victim's grades dropped during the 2003–2004 school year and he was withdrawing from his parents. His parents threatened to send him to a boarding or juvenile detention facility if he did not improve during summer school in 2004. The victim ran away from home several times that summer, leading his frustrated parents to enroll him in a boot camp program. When they told him about the enrollment, he ran away again—the day before he was taken to the program in a remote area of Missouri. The 5-month program describes itself as a boot camp and boarding school. Because it is a private facility, the state in which it is located does not require a license. According to Internet documents, the program costs almost $23,000 (or about $164 per day).

Investigative documents we reviewed indicate that at the time the parents enrolled the teenager, he did not have any issues in his medical history. Staff logs indicate that the victim was considered to be a continuous problem from the time he entered the program—he did not adhere to program rules and was otherwise noncompliant. By the second day of the boot camp phase of the program, staff noticed that the victim exhibited an oozing bump on his arm. School records and state investigation reports showed that the victim subsequently began to complain of muscle soreness, stumbled frequently, and vomited. As days passed, students noticed the victim was not acting normally, and reported that he defecated involuntarily on more than one occasion, including in the shower. Staff notes confirmed that the victim defecated and urinated on himself numerous times. Although he was reported to have fallen frequently and told staff he was feeling weak or ill, the staff interpreted this as being rebellious. The victim was "taken down"—forced to the floor and held there—on more than one occasion for misbehaving, according to documents we reviewed. Staff also tied a 20-pound sandbag around the victim's neck when he was too sick to exercise, forcing him to carry it around with him and not permitting him to sit down. Staff finally placed him in the "sick bay" in the morning on the day that he died. By midafternoon of that day, a staff member checking on him intermittently found the victim without a pulse. He yelled for assistance from other staff members, calling the school medical officer and the program owners. A responding staff member began CPR. The program medical officer called 9-1-1 after she arrived in the sick bay. An ambulance arrived about 30 minutes after the 9-1-1 call and transported the victim to a nearby hospital, where he was pronounced dead.

The victim died from complications of rhabdomyolysis due to a probable spider bite, according to the medical examiner's report.[8] A multiagency investigation was launched by state and local parties in the aftermath of the death. The state social services' abuse investigation determined that staff did not recognize the victim's medical distress or provide adequate treatment for the victim's bite. Although the investigation found evidence of staff neglect and concluded that earlier medical treatment may have prevented the death of the victim, no criminal charges were filed against the program, its owners, or any staff. The state also found indications that documents submitted by the program during the investigation may have been altered. The family of the victim filed a civil suit against the program and several of its staff in 2005 and settled out of court for $1 million, according to the judge.

This program is open and operating. The tuition is currently $4,500 per month plus a $2,500 "start-up fee." The program owner claims to have 25 years of experience working with children and teenagers. Members of her family also operate a referral program and a transport service out of program offices located separately from the actual program facility. During the course of our review, we found that current and former employees with this program filed abuse complaints with the local law enforcement agency but that no criminal investigation has been undertaken.

Mr. Chairman and Members of the Committee, this concludes my statement. We would be pleased to answer any questions that you may have at this time.

End Notes

[1] According to the Administration for Children and Families (part of the U.S. Department of Health and Human Services), NCANDS is a voluntary national data collection and analysis system created in response to the requirements of the Child Abuse Prevention and Treatment Act.

[2] For addition information, see H. T. Ireys, L. Achman, and A. Takyi. *State Regulation of Residential Facilities for Children with Mental Illness*. DHHS Pub. No. (SMA) 06-4167 (Rockville, Md.: Center for Mental Health Services, Substance Abuse and Mental Health Services Administration, 2006).

[3] Under Titles IV-B and IV-E of the Social Security Act and the Child Abuse and Neglect Prevention and Treatment Act.

[4] The program consisted of four phases. At the start of the second phase, students were required to fast for 2 days. During this phase, students slept under tarpaulins and, at the end of their fast, they were each given a supply of food and told that they were responsible for cooking and rationing it themselves. This food supply was the same for all participants and was supposed to last each of them for a week.

[5] Cutting is a common practice of superficially cutting oneself to draw attention and is often associated with adolescent mental health and behavioral issues. It is not considered an attempt to commit suicide, based on information in the American Psychiatric Association's 2003 Practice Guidelines for the Assessment and Treatment of Patients with Suicidal Behaviors.

[6] This is according to information from the U.S. National Library of Medicine, National Institutes of Health.

[7] According to its Web site, the Joint Commission on Health Care Organizations evaluates and accredits nearly 15,000 health care organizations and programs in the United States. It maintains state-of-the-art standards that focus on improving the quality and safety of care provided by health care organizations. Its comprehensive accreditation process evaluates an organization's compliance with these standards and other accreditation requirements.

[8] According to the National Library of Medicine, rhabdomyolysis is the breakdown of muscle fibers resulting in the release of muscle fiber contents into the bloodstream.

In: When Abuse and Neglect Occur at Residential... ISBN: 978-1-60876-965-0
Editor: Kirsten S. Madsen pp. 89-94

Chapter 4

CHILD ABUSE AND DECEPTIVE MARKETING BY RESIDENTIAL PROGRAMS FOR TEENS*

Christopher Belloncí

Mr. Chairman and members of the committee, my name is Christopher Bellonci, M.D. and I am pleased to be here in support of your proposed legislation, the "Stop Child Abuse in Residential Programs for Teens Act of 2008". I am a board-certified child and adolescent psychiatrist and the medical director at Walker, a multi-service agency in Needham, Massachusetts that offers residential treatment as one of a range of programs in our service array. I am a member of the American Academy of Child and Adolescent Psychiatry who paid for my travel to be here today. I co-wrote the Academy's Practice Parameter on The Prevention and Management of Aggressive Behavior in Child and Adolescent Psychiatric Institutions with Special Reference to Seclusion and Restraint and am a board member of the American Association of Children's Residential Centers.

First let me start by saying that treatment for a child or adolescent with serious emotional disturbance should be in the least restrictive environment, preferably with their family. However, there are many children that can not effectively be treated and managed in a home or community environment safely and need more acute intensive treatment. I am here today to talk about

---

* This is an edited, reformatted and augmented version of a U. S. House Committee Office publication dated April 24, 2008.

Walker and the specific needs of children and adolescents being treated in residential centers. We are licensed in Massachusetts through our state's Early Education and Care (EEC) agency. As an accredited school, we are also approved by our state Department of Education. We are accredited by the Council on Accreditation, a national accrediting body originally affiliated with the Child Welfare League of America.

Our licensing and accrediting agencies all require frequent renewal and on-sight visits by representatives of these various regulatory bodies. We also adhere to reporting requirements that are consistent with those proposed in your legislation. EEC has clear guidelines for adherence to civil rights that would prohibit restriction of access to mail, family visits or phone calls. We do not utilize wilderness programming or boot camp experiences. Our staff undergo a minimum of two weeks of preservice training including instruction in Cornell University's Therapeutic Crisis Intervention with a focus on de-escalation strategies and techniques that are individualized to the unique strengths and needs of the children we work with. Staff are cleared by the Massachusetts Criminal Records search process before they are allowed unsupervised contact with children. During orientation staff also receive training regarding mandated reporting laws, first aid and CPR. Walker has explicit policies outlining unacceptable forms of discipline consistent with those outlined in your proposed legislation. We also have clear policies regarding notification of adverse outcomes both to parents and guardians, as well as our state child protective service, our licensor, and funding and referral sources.

We strive for transparency in our work and view parents as essential allies in the complex treatment of children. We have an open campus and invite and encourage parents to visit and be an active part of the treatment milieu. Increasingly, we have been serving children and families in their homes, schools and communities. We actively partner with our state's child welfare and mental health departments in advancing best practice principles and provide consultation and program review and development to over 35 school districts in Massachusetts.

We take our commitment to family-driven practice seriously and in the last year have hired our first parent liaison coordinator, a parent of a child formerly in residential care at Walker. For over 5 years we have had a current parent serve as a voting member of our Board of Directors. We also have an active parent council and run parent support groups for all interested families.

I work directly with most of the children served in our residential program providing psychiatric treatment. It is against my ethical and licensing requirements to make a medication change without first discussing the risks and benefits of the proposed treatment and obtaining informed consent. In this regard, I am concerned that your legislation may not go far enough as it calls for notification to parents within 24 hours of a medication change when it is quite clear standards of ethical practice require the informed consent to be obtained prior to any removal or addition of a medication except in emergency situations.

The goal of this legislation is to ensure that children are not abused in these treatment settings, not to limit access to appropriate, regulated and licensed residential care for children who are in need of these services. All of us working in licensed residential centers should support this goal. All residential treatment programs should:

1. provide for all of the child's developmental needs including, mental health care, physical health care and education needs,
2. be licensed within the States where they practice and adhere to national standards,
3. encourage parents to be active parts of the treatment teams for their youth,
4. and employ a well trained, multidisciplinary, culturally competent staff.

The Board of the AACRC is equally concerned about the growing number of unlicensed residential programs. We believe that residential care in licensed and accredited facilities is an important and necessary part of an organized system of care and believe that all residential providers should be licensed within the States where they practice. In fact, all members of the AACRC are licensed and this is a condition of membership. We also strongly encourage residential centers to seek accreditation which hold the standards they must adhere to even higher.

As an organization representing agencies committed to working collaboratively with families and youth, we were disturbed by the concerns raised in this committee's previous hearing about children and youth experiencing harm in residential settings. We support the initiatives of this committee and its proposed legislation and believe that residential treatment is an appropriate placement for some youngsters and that there are high quality programs being administered by committed and competent staff.

The AACRC's mission is to support the professional development of this committed and competent workforce. The AACRC looks forward to working alongside this committee and state and federal agencies in ensuring that standards are in place for residential centers.

Licensing creates a baseline of expectations to which all programs within a state can be held accountable. Effective licensing requirements help promote client rights, staff competence, quality improvement, and consistent practice. They provide the constants, the solid ground from which innovative and transformative practice can be launched. They also provide a degree of safeguard against the potential of harm to children, events of a type that can undermine efforts to create meaningful change. AACRC requires licensure of its members and is concerned about the variability of practice that can occur in unlicensed settings, which can lead to adverse outcomes for children and their families and criticism of the field. AACRC encourages organizations to work with their state authorities to create meaningful and reasonable licensing frameworks for residentially based services.

Accreditation is not an effective replacement for licensing, as the accountability it yields is less stringent than that which typically occurs through licensing and regulation. Nonetheless it is an important accompaniment to licensure. Accreditation standards encompass emerging knowledge and evidence in the field and come together to define clinical and managerial practices that result in high quality and effective care.

Agency-developed standards, policies, and procedures build upon the framework of licensing and accreditation, creating unique, mission-driven structures as the foundation for care and innovation. Establishment and measurement of desired outcomes and performance indicators helps each organization assess the degree to which it is fulfilling its own objectives and creates the possibility of comparison or benchmarking with other similar entities on key aspects of care identified through accreditation and licensing.

Compliance with accreditation standards, particularly in conjunction with adherence to licensing and regulatory requirements and a quality improvement infrastructure, provides the foundation of safety and best practice that can infuse transformational change, elevate practice, and improve outcomes. AACRC supports efforts to establish licensure requirements and encourages agencies to pursue voluntary accreditation, as part of implementing a transformation agenda.

In the last two decades, the thinking about family involvement across the child serving systems has begun to change. The Child and Adolescent Service System Program (1985) envisioned a central role for families in community systems of care for children with mental health problems. Wraparound, family decision making, and parent-professional partnerships have emerged in child welfare, education, medical, and juvenile justice arenas, as well as in mental health. Such service configurations have recently been supported by research and heralded in salient mental health public policy studies, including the Surgeon General's and the President's New Freedom Commission reports. Research specific to residential care has also consistently identified improved child outcomes when parents and families are more involved. The response from the field to these developments has been slow but not insignificant, as residential centers across the country increasingly design processes and practices for more inclusion of parents and family members in the care of their children. The result has been improved outcomes for children and families.

Parents and families provide important information and feedback. An approach that engages them equally creates a shared responsibility for growth and change. It provides the opportunity for staff to work together with parents and to utilize family members' experience and expertise. This yields an increased ability to understand the child within the context of his/her family, culture and community, and to develop realistic expectations, plans, and supports. The family is affirmed in having their strengths recognized and valued; the staff benefit from having support and assistance and from being relieved of the implicit, at times self-imposed, responsibility to be the ones who will "fix" the child. Family-driven care is a partnership.

Parents are strong and effective voices, advocating in pragmatic and realistic ways for the needs of children on quality improvement, planning, and governance bodies. As political partners with professionals, parents are powerful advocates for the full continuum of care, inclusive of residential, and for efforts to meet the needs of children and families in local communities. The research in residential treatment consistently shows that the processes and outcomes of care improve in correlation with the degree of family involvement.

At the governance level parents are valuable members of Boards of Directors, and offer critical input into strategic planning and resource allocation. At the system level parents can have important voices on advisory committees and interagency collaboratives. Parents understand the importance of a full array of services and, in telling their stories, have a powerful influence on policy makers.

Such multi-level partnerships can help establish and reinforce a culture of family-driven care. They are more readily supported if the organization has made the leadership commitment to become family driven and can dedicate budgetary resources to supporting parent travel, paying stipends, or hiring parents as paid staff. The Board of Directors and CEO can ask themselves a series of key questions in assessing readiness to move in this direction, for example:

- *Do the staff of the organization act, speak, and interact in ways that truly welcome, support, affirm, and incorporate the perspectives and wishes of parents?*

- *Do parents have to be "invited" into the organization or is it a baseline assumption of staff that parents are reciprocal partners?*

- *Is the organization committed to redefining itself as providing an intervention within a community continuum rather than as a placement of last resort?*

- *Does the organization believe that sharing decision-making, leadership, and power with parents yields better outcomes for children and youth?*

- *Is the organization willing to implement training and other practices that culturally reinforce the importance of parents and families in day to day actions, discussions, and care planning?*

The responses to these questions can drive strategic planning and practice innovation. Changes in practice, even incremental, can and do lead to positive results.

The American Academy of Child and Adolescent Psychiatry is currently working on a Practice Parameter defining best practice for residential treatment and once available, AACAP would be happy to share it with the committee. Many of my remarks are taken from Position Papers developed over the last 5 years by the AACRC.

Thank you for the opportunity to present these comments to the Committee.

In: When Abuse and Neglect Occur at Residential... ISBN: 978-1-60876-965-0
Editor: Kirsten S. Madsen pp.95-99

Chapter 5

CHILD ABUSE AND DECEPTIVE MARKETING BY RESIDENTIAL PROGRAMS FOR TEENS*

Jon Martin-Crawford

I would like to thank the Chairman and the Committee for the opportunity to present my side of this story. After watching the hearing back in October, I was inspired by the clear case of morality that brought together both sides of the aisle in this discussion.

We have been called "noisy complainers" we have been called "manipulating troublemakers." After over 10 years, I finally have my chance to speak. My name is Jon Martin-Crawford. I was locked up at the NATSAP affiliated program, The Family Foundation School, in Hancock, NY, from 1995 to 1997.

My life at home was anything but stable. This caused me to seek my own release from it all. I created a persona for myself at school, the troublemaker, always looking for the attention I didn't get at home. Involved in drugs by the age of 13, I was lost. I was constantly in trouble, and in a lot of fights. Bomb scares, drugs, suspensions and expulsions from school certainly had my parents worried, at wit's end, and desperate for a solution. My only release was my music, my writing, and my skateboarding. After being expelled from public school and one private school for marijuana and writing an

---

* This is an edited, reformatted and augmented version of a U. S. Government Committee Office publication dated April 24, 2008.

underground newspaper, my parents sent me to The Family shortly thereafter. Here, they thought, after touring the facility, I would get better, and be able to live a normal life again. They thought this was the best thing they could be doing for me...for our family.

Once I arrived at The Family, I knew I was there until I was 18. I hated my parents at that point and tried to leave, until three 6foot plus 250lb plus men forced me to sit and I saw that I had no choice. I went through what seems like the ritualistic stripping of clothes, self and identity almost all of us survivors faced. My clothes were taken and thrown away. My music, my art, my skateboard all destroyed. What I didn't have with me, my parents were told to destroy as well. I was left with only a letter from my mother for the next 3 months.

I had been to some inpatient settings before, but this one was different. Other places allowed phone calls, mail, and peer communication. Here, I wasn't even allowed to call home the first few months. Even after that, I only got that one phone call home a week...nothing more... no access to Child Protective Services. Here I was only allowed to talk to staff and kids that had been there more than 6 months. I was told I was denying the extent of my drug use, and I was confused as to just how I would "get better" enough to just see my family. I sat and watched, and learned to play the game of lies necessary to get privileges, and eventually get out. I got lucky and figured these rules out quickly enough to not endure what I saw many kids endure. But I still witnessed it all. Including:

1 Staff punching students in the face while restraining.....not once but several times
2 Typical restraint procedures were wrapping kids up in Duct tape and blankets. Kids were not let out of this wrap, even to use the bathroom, feminine hygiene, or just to move around and let the body out of the confinement, while in an isolation room (the 6X6 library room)
3 Restraints were not only done by faculty, but many senior and junior members of students. Usually, this was even more brutal and was often done in front of all other students to show "what will happen if you act out"
4 Kids forced to eat food they were allergic to, and keep eating even if vomiting as a result.
5 Kids as young as 12 being taken out of school to carry out pointless manual labor such as shovel manure, carry wheelbarrows of rocks, sweeping the roof, etc. for days on end

6 When kids tried to run away it was again, not only staff, but many students told to chase, tackle, restrain, and bring them back.
7 Many things heard from staff, berating kids with high level verbal abuse, often of a highly derogatory and sexual nature, at times regarding sexual orientation
8 An admitted sex addict was one of the high-up faculty and counselors, as well as a dorm monitor living above the boy's dorm

The rules I learned to avoid much of these problems were as follows:

1 Make up a horrible past to "cure yourself of"... our moral inventory was nearly always fabricated to make our problems seem worse, and the program seem like salvation
2 Tell on yourself and your peers for things you may have never done to give the illusion you're getting better
3 If you have certain "gifts" you can find ways to skate by. Me, I was the school's golden boy with my pen and my graduation speech, as well as others were used as propaganda at graduations as part of "family day" for all parents to hear.
4 Under no circumstances tell your parents or prospective parents the truth about what you see happening.

Yes, I was fortunate enough to go home once a month after a while. All I wanted for those weekends at home was to sleep, relax, and watch television. I quickly learned that telling our parents the truth about what happened at The Family would only be explained away as manipulation and we would lose our privileges.

While I had been fortunate enough to miss out on most of the horrors personally, I unfortunately gave many tours to prospective parents, always omitting the details of restraints, punishments, and lack of any sort of communication or safeguards against the abuses that took place. As a dorm leader, I was told to wake up one of the kids in my dorm with the light from the lamp... that only had a flood light as a bulb... burning his retina. I participated in the restraining, and took part in the barrage of verbal attacks just as did many of my peers. I am not proud of this, but we had no choice in any of this. If we did not conform, we were "being negative" and subject to the same treatment and lack of privileges.

Once I left, however, I saw that I was now in the real world with real problems again, and the school had never helped me with those problems.

After nightmares of The Family led to a relapse, I was soon out of Vassar College and into the military. The training in the military, although viewed by some to be harsh, was a cakewalk compared to the hell endured at The Family School. My trust issues were never resolved after leaving The Family, and the nightmares remained. Ultimately, all these psychological flashbacks led to the need for my discharge from the Army, something I regret to this day.

For years, I thought all this was my fault. While the nightmares and anxiety never wore off, getting high made it go away again. I will not blame others for my choices, my mistakes. I take responsibility for those. What I do blame The Family for is stripping me of my childhood. I still have nightmares of being locked up and told I'm ruining my life. I still read the monthly paper of lies the school puts out and get nauseous remembering the stuff we witnessed.

The only thing I can say to temper my disdain for these types of schools, or at least for The Family is this:

While the programs, as they are, have little positive effect long term, I do believe that kids in my position need some sort of help. I do believe there can be a safe solution, as some staff are genuinely decent and caring people We need oversight and regulation of these facilities with swift and severe penalties for those who stray from the standards.

What must be remembered through all of this is that the "success stories" of programs tend to fall in the one to two year range after leaving such program. ..and usually are the opinions of parents. A true statistic? Of the 25 kids from my graduating class and the one prior to mine, maybe 4 remained sober. While many can now say they live successful lives, it came anywhere between 5-10 years after leaving the program and figuring out life on their own with psychiatric help. Unfortunately, this cannot be said for all.

The programs are quick to take credit for a successful story, and are just as fast to claim anyone that doesn't make it just "didn't work the program" The truth? The nightmares and psychological scars of being dragged from your home to a place in the middle of nowhere, restrained in blankets and duct tape, assaulted, verbally and physically.. ..those scars and that trauma never go away.

For my parents, who thought that my time at The Family was the best thing they could do, I hope they understand I do not blame them for what I've been through. I know the pain I put them through, and the desperation they faced. I know they did what they thought would help me the most. They were lied to, or at least not told the whole truth...it was not their fault. I know it's hard to tell sometimes, but it was not bad parenting that led to this decision. It was good parenting and deceptive tours and marketing. While I may have received a more focused education, every other part of my teenage life, and early adult life, was stunted as a result of my time at The Family. Fortunately, today, my relationship with my family is better than it's ever been. I have the mutual respect of both my parents despite our differences in opinion at times. While this topic often causes some pain, I know that what they chose was out of love. What they got was something they never could have imagined...or believed until now.

For my friends who have since died from suicide, and still suffer the nightmares, our time and our voice will not be in vain. There comes a time for every man to make amends and right their wrongs. This is a lesson these programs preach, and it is a lesson they must now follow.

In: When Abuse and Neglect Occur at Residential... ISBN: 978-1-60876-965-0
Editor: Kirsten S. Madsen pp.101-104

Chapter 6

CHILD ABUSE AND DECEPTIVE MARKETING BY RESIDENTIAL PROGRAMS FOR TEENS*

George Miller

WASHINGTON, D.C. – *Below are the prepared remarks of U.S. Rep. George Miller (D-CA), the chairman of the House Education and Labor Committee, for a committee hearing on "Child Abuse and Deceptive Marketing by Residential Programs for Teens."*

Good morning. Welcome to today's hearing on "Child Abuse and Deceptive Marketing by Residential Programs for Teens."

Last October, this Committee heard from the parents of three children who died in private residential programs as a result of the abuse and neglect they experienced at the hands of staff members.

The stories these parents told left everyone in this room stunned, heartbroken, and angry.

Bob Bacon testified that program staff members mocked his son, Aaron, when the 16-year-old boy asked for medical help, calling him a "faker." For weeks, the staff deprived Aaron of adequate food and water – even when his weight loss became frighteningly apparent.

---

* This is an edited, reformatted and augmented version of a U. S. Government House of Representatives publication dated April 24, 2008.

Cynthia Harvey told the committee that program staff members waited 45 minutes before summoning appropriate medical care for her daughter, Erica, who had collapsed and was having difficulty breathing.

Paul Lewis testified that program staff members ignored his son Ryan's obvious signs of emotional distress, denying him the psychiatric care that could have saved his life.

In each of the three cases, it was clear from the parents' testimony that the deaths of their children were preventable. Untrained and uncaring staff, reckless management, and irresponsible operating practices permitted these horrible tragedies to occur.

Sadly, the deaths of Aaron, Erica, and Ryan were not isolated cases.

The Government Accountability Office found thousands of allegations of abuse and neglect at private residential programs for teens between 1990 and 2007.

The abuses included staff members forcing children to remain in so-called "stress" positions for hours at a time; to undergo extreme physical exertion without food, water, or rest; and to eat their own vomit.

The purpose of today's hearing is to gain a better overall understanding of the industry in which these types of abuses have been allowed, in many cases, to continue almost unchecked.

Specifically, we will learn more about where these programs operate, the loose patchwork of state laws that govern them, and how they market themselves to parents.

We will also discuss legislation that Congresswoman McCarthy and I have introduced to keep kids safe in residential programs.

Residential programs for teens – which come in a variety of forms, including therapeutic boarding schools, wilderness camps, boot camps, and behavior modification facilities – have sprung up in greater numbers since the 1990s.

As we will hear today, a number of these programs use deceptive marketing practices to appeal to parents.

They claim to be subject to independent inspections that never happen.

They claim to offer services that they don't, like schooling with transferable education credits.

They assure parents that health insurance will cover the cost of their services when in reality it won't.

Programs are aided in these deceptions by their relationships to ancillary service providers, like referral services.

While referral services purport to offer independent advice to parents about which programs would be best for their children, the truth is that at least some of the referral services operate with significant conflicts of interest.

This tangled web of deception, fraud, and conflicts of interest makes it extremely difficult for parents to judge whether any of these programs offer a safe, professional, high-quality environment for their children.

We know that there are many programs and many people around the country who are committed to helping improve the lives of young people and who do good work every day, but it is difficult for parents to tell the good programs from the bad.

Making matters worse, these programs often operate free of minimum standards of care. It is estimated that hundreds of the programs operate nationwide, with anywhere from no regulation whatsoever to some regulation.

Even the information that states collect on many of these programs is limited. Indeed, in a survey conducted by the GAO, state agencies in 45 states could not say whether deaths had occurred at exclusively private residential programs for teens in 2006.

The legislation that Congresswoman McCarthy and I have introduced will end the federal government's longstanding failure to address this nightmare of abuse and neglect.

The goal of our legislation is simple – we want to keep children safe.

The legislation will require the U.S. Department of Health and Human Services to establish minimum standards that all programs must meet, including prohibitions on the physical and mental abuse of children and requirements that programs provide children with adequate food, water, and medical care.

These standards will also include new training requirements for program staff members, including how to identify and report child abuse.

The legislation will require HHS to set up a hotline for people to call to report abuse at these programs. It will also require HHS to create a web site with information about each program, so that parents can look to see if substantiated cases of abuse have occurred at a program that they are considering for their kids.

The legislation will require HHS to enforce these standards by inspecting program facilities and, when there are violations, by issuing civil penalties of up to $50,000 per violation. Within three years, the legislation would call upon the states to take up this role of setting standards and enforcing them.

We have an obligation to keep kids safe no matter what setting they are in, and this legislation would take the first step toward finally ending the horrific abuses that have gone on for too long in private residential programs for teens.

We must treat this issue with the urgency it demands by acting on this legislation quickly.

Individuals who have themselves lived through this abuse are in the hearing room today, as are family members of abuse victims. I want to thank you all for being here to remind us why this issue is so important.

I also want to thank all of our witnesses. We appreciate that you took the time to be with us today and we look forward to hearing your testimony.

Thank you.

http://edlabor.house.gov

In: When Abuse and Neglect Occur at Residential... ISBN: 978-1-60876-965-0
Editor: Kirsten S. Madsen pp.105-110

Chapter 7

CHILD ABUSE AND DECEPTIVE MARKETING BY RESIDENTIAL PROGRAMS FOR TEENS*

Kathryn Whitehead

Good morning Chairman Miller, Ranking Member McKeon and distinguished members of the Committee. Thank you for this opportunity to testify before you today. I appreciate your leadership and efforts to help protect youth from abuse and neglect by convening this hearing.

I am here to share the tragic experience of myself and family at an unregulated facility in Montana called Mission Mountain School. I am also here to tell you about the patterns of mistreatment and abuse of youth in residential programs across the country, which I have become aware of through my work with the youth advocacy group, Community Alliance for the Ethical Treatment of Youth. Finally, I will offer my perspective on the ways in which legislation could help to increase protections and at long last bring an end to the atrocious mistreatment of American youth in residential facilities across the country.

My story is one of a youth battling mental illness, a group of Montana residents taking the liberty to assume that their own experience as recovering alcoholics was qualification enough to operate a facility for struggling youth, and parents operating from a place of gullible desperation, willing to spend

* This is an edited, reformatted and augmented version of a U. S. Government Committee Office publication dated April 24, 2008.

upwards of $70,000 to fund a fictitious therapeutic milieu that amounted to little more than humiliation, deprivation and abuse – leaving in its wake a family torn apart and a traumatized 15 year old.

At the age of 13 I was diagnosed with chronic depression following a suicide attempt, and hospitalized at a local psychiatric hospital. When I was discharged, lacking any community based support, my family sought to identify services outside of my community and found Mission Mountain School at the recommendation of a hired educational consultant.

Mission Mountain School held great promise, as it was sold to us as a small family-like therapeutic environment for girls ages 12-18 with above average intelligence. It was located in picturesque Condon MT. Though I felt unspeakable grief at leaving my family and all that was familiar to me behind, I knew I needed help. I packed my treasured belongings, reminders of home, and my mom and I flew out to MT. I felt hopeful, that maybe this 'special school' for kids like me would help me, as they claimed to have the ability to treat any myriad of serious psychiatric issues, such as bipolar disorder, eating disorders and depression.

Sadly, this could not be further from the truth. Upon arrival I quickly encountered the punitive and invasive interventions, which would come to define my 18 months at Mission Mountain School.

My mom left me shortly after we had arrived and my belongings were taken from me. I never received any explanation of the rules of the program, though the rules quickly took shape during the series of groups sessions held daily. Everyone was called out in group when they first arrived - every infraction was framed as an act of dishonesty. We were all labeled "liars" and "manipulators" upon arrival. Our daily diaries were read, and compared to the detailed life histories that we were forced to write soon after arrival, which were required to include details of every sexual encounter we had experienced in our short lives to ensure accuracy.

Often there were 'punishments' when we were thought to have been dishonest, euphemistically called "consequences." Consequence always involved some type of physical punishment – forced labor, such as ice picking, rock picking, and chopping wood. More "serious" rule breaking would result in what was called an "intervention," which was work crew all day long with breaks only during group, chores and mealtime.

Sometimes the group was put on "interventions" which would last for weeks if not months, and during this time no contact was allowed with the outside. It was generally understood that we were being exhausted for the purpose of making us more truthful – whatever that meant to those in charge.

Exercise was a rigorous daily requirement. Slowing down from exhaustion only resulted in more exercise or getting yelled at.

I was not allowed to speak with my family for months after I arrived, and calls thereafter were monitored. Any criticisms were labeled as "manipulative" and my phone call was promptly disconnected, followed by punishment. If at some point we "advanced" enough in the program to not require such monitoring, that just meant that by that point, we were no longer expressing our concerns because we knew our parents wouldn't believe us anyway.

The most powerful figure at the facility was the headmaster who has no formal training in mental health and whose group therapy sessions were particularly bizarre and frightening. He was often confrontational or would smirk and laugh. He would pit friends against friends, and force us to say mean things to one another. He would attempt to unearth repressed memories and encourage regressive states. I recall that on multiple occasions my friends speaking as if they were toddlers, recounting alleged instances of abuse. Hours would be spent with girls reliving their traumatic experiences at the unqualified hands of the staff. Intensive group sessions sometimes lasted all night. Bathroom use was heavily regulated. Any allegations of abuse discussed in group "therapy" were never reported by staff to proper authorities.

Because all of the founders were members of AA, it seemed to them that everyone was an addict of sorts. I was deemed an alcoholic and sex addict, a close friend was deemed a sex addict. She had never had sex in her life, and denied the claim and as a result, staff forced her to carry 6 large rocks on her back at all times for several months, naming them issues like "sexual abuse" and "sex addiction," until she conceded to staff that each issue was true, detailing traumatizing experiences supportive of that claim. When I got caught with a plan to run away I was placed on personal intervention where I had to rock pick for a week, eight to ten hours a day, at one point dropped off 25 miles from school and forced to hike back. This was all done in the name of therapy.

At other times inappropriate and humiliating interventions were used such as forbidding youth from talking for several weeks at a time, forcing youth to wear gloves because it was thought that they masturbated, or tying two girls together because two girls didn't get along. Claims of illness were framed as manipulative.

Education was non-existent; schooling a joke. We would have schooling maybe a few hours a day a couple days out of the week. I taught myself algebra, and uncertified teachers taught English and Spanish. We weren't allowed any information about the outside word such as newspapers or news magazines. I learned next to nothing. It wasn't until I was nearing graduation from Mission Mountain School that I underwent testing outside of the facility and was diagnosed with a learning disability.

We had no access to advocates, no rights whatsoever. Groups of educational consultants would come in on occasion for a visit. They were always impressed by our manners and ability to be so forthcoming. None came to the facility unannounced. None asked us for our honest opinions of the program... although even if they had, given the insidious fear-based environment, it's doubtful I would've spoken – it wasn't long before I was broken down and I came to believe what I was told: that Mission Mountain School was to be the only place that could save me from myself or I'd end up in "jail, insane or dead". The cumulative effect of the program was losing all sense of self.

Then one day, 18 months later, I was told I was to be discharged. None of it made any sense to me – though I was told I had been given the tools to live, I found it difficult to reconcile their claim with my internal landscape. My nights were filled with a reoccurring nightmare of being chased by the founders and brought back to the facility, despite my protests explaining that I was healthy now. In the end, all Mission Mountain School gave me was more confusion, increased anxiety and depression, and made social functioning after discharge evermore difficult. It wasn't until 10 years later that I came to recognize the damage done and sought change.

I'd like to speak about the work I've done since then, which will hopefully speak to the broad pattern of atrocities Dr. Pinto commented on in her testimony at the hearings in October 2007. As co-founder and Executive Director of the Community Alliance for the Ethical Treatment of Youth, I have heard from over one thousand survivors and understand that, in most instances, parents remain unaware of the abuse their children have experienced and often firmly believe the program saved their child life. To me, this is the saddest repercussion of these facilities. At once not only is the trust between parent and child broken, but the truth of the youth is further hidden behind a façade promulgated by deceived parents. In my communications the majority of folks I've been in contact with have reported first hand with regards to:

- Trauma due to use of escort services
- Communication and privacy rights violations such as mail-monitoring, call- monitoring and filtering, restricted or interrupted correspondence.
- Inappropriate Seclusion and Restraint

- Inhumane Treatment such as:
  - Forced labor
  - Restricted access to the bathroom
  - Scare tactics
  - Exposure to harsh elements
  - Excessive exercise
  - Food/nutritional deprivation
  - Sleep deprivation
  - Physical punishment
  - Emotional, physical or sexual abused by staff
- Education and Mental Health Treatment
  - no individualized plan
  - dissatisfaction with the training background of the staff members who were providing education, therapy, support and/or care

What I am hoping to convey today through my testimony is that numerous residential facilities that are in operation today are stripping youth of their basic human rights to dignity, respect, to least restrictive care, appropriate mental health treatment, to education and parental contact, to freedom of thought, opinion and association, and ultimately to freedom from censorship and torture. The legitimate practice of therapeutic intervention is being injected with a perverse form of social control, including inhumane treatment and practices, which defy the ethical principles upheld by peer reviewed mental health practices.

As a nation it is our obligation to hold places of care accountable to their claim. A nation with the best interest of the child in mind must be in the position to assure this is occurring. For this reason it is critical that oversight is stringent enough for this to occur, it is questionable that youth safety can be assured if visits occur once every 2 years. Quality assurance is paramount – if a place claims to be a place of healing a facility must be able to back up such claims. It is our nations responsibility to families to ensure not just that abuse is not occurring, but that therapy is never used as justification for the violation of the human rights of youth. Consistent with such commitment, every youth ought be entitled to the least restrictive care possible. Facilities must be held accountable to claims that deceive parents into thinking that no alternative exists and that years of imprisonment are a necessary therapeutic intervention. Of concern are misinformed families who lack community support and feel they have no alternative but to choose institutionalize their child (unnecessarily) at the behest of programs concerned with their interests over that of the youth.

I strongly believe this bill to be a promising and important first step in curbing such draconian methodology this industry has been founded upon and applaud Chairman Miller for introducing the first piece of comprehensive legislation to that end.

In: When Abuse and Neglect Occur at Residential... ISBN: 978-1-60876-965-0
Editor: Kirsten S. Madsen pp.111-117

Chapter 8

CONSIDERING A PRIVATE RESIDENTIAL TREATMENT PROGRAM FOR A TROUBLED TEEN? QUESTIONS FOR PARENTS AND GUARDIANS TO ASK*

Federal Trade Commission

Private residential treatment programs for young people offer a range of services, including drug and alcohol treatment, confidence building, military-style and psychological counseling for a variety of addiction, behavioral, and emotional problems. Many of these programs are intended to provide a less-restrictive alternative to incarceration or hospitalization, or an intervention for a troubled young person.

If you are a parent or guardian and think you have exhausted intervention alternatives for a troubled teen, you may be considering a private residential treatment program. These programs go by a variety of names, including "therapeutic boarding schools," "emotional growth academies," "teen boot camps," "behavior modification facilities," and "wilderness therapy programs."

No standard definitions exist for specific types of programs. The programs are not regulated by the federal government, and many are not subject to state

* This is an edited, reformatted and augmented version of a Federal Trade Commission publication dated July 2008.

licensing or monitoring as mental health or educational facilities, either. A 2007 Report to Congress by the Government Accountability Office (GAO) found cases involving serious abuse and neglect at some of these programs. Many programs advertise on the Internet and through other media, making claims about staff credentials, the level of treatment a participant will receive, program accreditation, education credit transfers, success rates, and endorsements by educational consultants.

The Federal Trade Commission (FTC), the nation's consumer protection agency, cautions that before you enroll a youngster in a private residential treatment program, check it out: ask questions; ask for proof or support for claims about staff credentials, program accreditation, and endorsements; do a site visit; and get all policies and promises in writing.

FACTS FOR CONSUMERS

Questions to Ask

Here are some questions to ask representatives of any program you may be considering. The responses may help you determine if the program is appropriate for your child.

1. Are you licensed by the state?

If the answer is yes, find out what aspects of the program the license covers: educational, mental/ behavioral health, and/or residential?

If the program claims to be licensed, get the name of the state agency that issued the license and contact the agency to verify that the license is current. Often, the licensing will be through a state Department of Health and Human Services or its equivalent. If the program's representative can't provide the name of the licensing agency, consider it a red flag.

If the program is unlicensed and you still want to consider it, contact the state Attorney General (www.naag.org), the Better Business Bureau (www.bbb.org), and the local consumer protection office (www.consumeraction.gov/state.shtml) where the program is located.

Regardless of whether a program is licensed, when contacting any of these groups:

- Ask for copies of all publicly available information, including any complaints or actions filed against the program, site visit evaluations, violations, and corrective actions.
- Pay particular attention to any reports of unsanitary or unsafe living conditions, nutritionally compromised diets, exposure to extreme environmental conditions or extreme physical exertion, inadequate staff supervision or a low ratio of staff to residents, medical neglect, physical or sexual abuse of youth by program staff or other residents, and any violation of youth or family rights.

2. Do you provide an academic curriculum? if so, is it available to all program participants? Do you have teachers who are certified or licensed by your state?

Some programs may offer only self-study or distance education. Sometimes, educational options are not made available until a resident has reached an advanced phase of the program. In addition, some programs may claim that academic credits will transfer to the resident's home school and count toward a high school diploma. Check with the board of education in the state where the program operates

- and with your state board if you live out-of-state
- to verify that academic credits will transfer.

3. What about accreditation?

Several independent nonprofit organizations, like the Joint Commission (JACHO), the Council on Accreditation (COA), and the Commission on Accreditation of Rehabilitation Facilities (CARF), accredit mental health programs and providers.

- JACHO accredits and certifies more than 15,000 health care organizations and programs in the U.S. (www.jointcommission.org)
- COA is an international child- and family- service and behavioral healthcare organization that accredits 38 different service areas, including substance abuse treatment, and more than 60 types of programs. (www.coanet.org)
- CARF International is an independent accreditor of human services providers in areas including behavioral health, child and youth services, and employment and community services. (www.carf.org)

Ask whether all components of the program are accredited, for example, the base program, the drug and alcohol component, and the wilderness program. Then contact the accrediting organization for confirmation.

The GAO's Report noted that one program claimed to be accredited by the JACHO, but in fact, only the base program was accredited. Neither the wilderness program nor the drug and alcohol component was accredited.

The organizations above grant accreditation and certification after evaluating the quality of services provided by a treatment program. Parents and guardians should be aware that some other organizations that claim to accredit schools may serve merely as membership organizations, and may not conduct site inspections or otherwise evaluate the quality of the programs they certify. If a treatment program claims to be certified or accredited, parents and guardians should contact the accrediting organization and ask about the standards the organization uses when issuing a certification.

4. Do you have a clinical director? What are his/ her credentials?

Typically, a clinical director is responsible for overseeing, supporting, and maintaining the quality of care for the program. A clinical director may have an advanced degree in a related field, like clinical psychology, and may be involved in providing individual therapy, assessment and consultation, staff training and development, and managing or supervising the components of the program.

5. What are the credentials of the staff, especially the counselors and therapists, who will be working with my child?

Do they have appropriate and relevant advanced degrees like a Masters in Social Work, a license to do clinical social work (LCSW), a Ph.D., or an M.D.? Are they certified or licensed within the state? If they are, by what agency or organization?

Ask to see copies of relevant documents, and consider contacting the certifying or licensing organization to confirm the staff credentials. The GAO found that some program leaders falsely claimed to have credentials in therapy or medicine, which led some parents to trust them with teens who had serious mental or physical disabilities requiring different levels of treatment.

6. How experienced is your staff? Have they worked at other residential treatment programs? if yes, where and for how long?

Ask to see current certifications in CPR and other emergency medicine. For wilderness programs, also ask for proof of relevant training and expertise.

7. Do you conduct background checks on your employees?

If the answer is yes, find out who does the background check and how extensive it is. Call the company to confirm that it provides background check services for the treatment program. If the answer is no or the program does not conduct background checks, consider it a red flag.

8. What are the criteria for admission ? Do you conduct pre-admission assessments? Are they in person, by phone, or over the internet? Who conducts them?

If your child has serious addiction problems or psychological issues, take special care to ensure that the program is equipped to deal with them. Discuss the appropriateness of the program with your child's psychologist, psychiatrist, or other healthcare provider.

9. Will you provide an individualized program with a detailed explanation of the therapies, interventions, and supports that will address my child's needs? When is this done? How often will my child be reassessed?

Ask whether your child will have group or individual therapy sessions. If the answer is yes, ask how often the sessions will take place and who will conduct them. Once enrolled, confirm with your child that the promised level of care is being received.

10. How do you handle medical issues like illness or injury? is there a nurse or doctor on staff? on the premises? Will you contact me? Will i be notified or consulted if there's a change in treatment or medication?

Ask for copies of procedures the program follows on dealing with medical emergencies.

11. How do you define success? What is your success rate? How is it measured?

Some programs make specific success claims in their advertising materials. To date, there is no systematic, independently collected descriptive or outcome data on these programs.

12. How do you discipline program participants?

Ask about policies and procedures for discipline.

13. Can I contact/speak with my child when I want? Can my child contact me when he wants?

Some programs prohibit, monitor, or otherwise restrict verbal or written communication between you and your child. Find out what is allowed and prohibited before you enroll your child.

14. What are the costs? What do they cover? What is your refund policy if the program doesn't work out?

Private residential treatment programs often charge hundreds of dollars per day. While health insurance sometimes may pay a limited amount, for the most part, the youngster's family is responsible for paying the fees and bills.

15. Do you have relationships with companies and individuals that provide educational and referral services?

Some companies may provide services, claiming to match troubled kids with an appropriate treatment program. Be aware that although some of these services represent themselves as independent, they may not be. They may actually be operated or paid by one or more of the treatment programs. Ask the service if it receives commissions from the treatment programs.

For More Information

Among the sources of information for families researching private residential treatment programs for troubled youngsters are:

- The Government Accountability Office's (GAO) Report to Congress: "Residential Treatment Programs: Concerns Regarding Abuse and

Death in Certain Programs for Troubled Youth" (October 2007) – www.gao.gov

- The U.S. Department of Health and Human Services, Centers for Disease Control and Prevention's list of state mental health agencies – www.cdc.gov/mentalhealth/state_orgs.htm
- The U.S. Department of State Fact Sheet: "Behavior Modification Facilities" – www.state.gov
- Your State Attorney General – www.naag.org
- The Alliance for the Safe, Therapeutic and Appropriate use of Residential Treatment (A START) – http://astart.fmhi.usf.edu A START is sponsored by the Department of Child and Family Studies of the University of South Florida. The Alliance includes leaders in psychology, psychiatry, nursing, mental health law, policy and family advocacy, as well as individuals with direct program experience as director, evaluator, parent, or participant in such programs.

About the FTC

The FTC works for the consumer to prevent fraudulent, deceptive, and unfair business practices in the marketplace and to provide information to help consumers spot, stop, and avoid them. To file a complaint or to get free information on consumer issues, visit ftc.gov or call toll-free, 1-877-FTC-HELP (1-877-382-4357); TTY: 1-866-653-4261. The FTC enters Internet, telemarketing, identity theft, and other fraud-related complaints into Consumer Sentinel, a secure online database available to hundreds of civil and criminal law enforcement agencies in the U.S. and abroad.

Federal Trade Commission
Bureau of Consumer Protection
Division of Consumer and Business Education
July 2008

In: When Abuse and Neglect Occur at Residential... ISBN: 978-1-60876-965-0
Editor: Kirsten S. Madsen pp.119-122

Chapter 9

COMMITTEE ON EDUCATION AND LABOR*

Bob Bacon

Chairman Miller and Distinguished Committee Members, My name is Bob Bacon, the father of Aaron Bacon.

Speaking for my wife, and Aaron's mother Sally, his brother Jarid and his sister Kia Sullivan; and speaking on behalf of the many families not at this table whose lives have been shattered by these fraudulent programs, we deeply appreciate your efforts to put a stop to this country's growing industry of institutionalized child abuse.

During our search for the best alternative to the remaining three months of Aaron's sophomore year in high school, my wife and I spoke with therapists, counselors, pastors and doctors until we were eventually referred by friends to North Star Expeditions, a now defunct, but formerly licensed Utah-based program that billed itself as a "wilderness therapy program for troubled teens."

After reading their very compelling brochure, speaking to their office by phone, and finally meeting the owners for a personal interview, we thought we had found the perfect situation: Caring people who were experienced in counseling kids who were struggling with drugs and social pressure – and to top it off - writing in a daily journal we were told was an integral part of their "counseling" program. As a writer, we felt journaling would help Aaron to sort

---

* This is an edited, reformatted and augmented version of a U. S. Government Committee Office publication dated October 10, 2007.

things out; and we were certain that, as a poet Aaron would find the awesome beauty of southern Utah to be inspirational and spiritually healing.

Of course, being normal, trusting and honest people ourselves– we assumed we were being told the truth. We were dead wrong. His mother and I will never escape our decision to send our gifted 16 year old son to his death at North Star. The guilt of our apparent naiveté was crippling. We were conned by their fraudulent claims, and will go to our graves regretting our gullibility.

Adding further to our regret, we were talked into using their escort service. Aaron was taken from his bed at 5:00 AM on Tuesday morning, March the 1st, 1994 by two burley strangers who announced to Aaron with a tone of authority that any resistance on his part would be countered with whatever physical force was necessary. He was not allowed to speak to us, or put on any shoes.

His eyes expressed a strange mixture of anger, despair, fear and loving sadness. I was able to manage only the briefest of hugs which, being restrained, he could not return. In the trauma of this surreal instant I offered words of comfort without thinking of their potentially ominous meaning when I said, "Aaron, I know you will find God in the wilderness." Little did I know that these would be the last words I would ever speak to my youngest son!

His mother managed only a fleeting moment to cradle his face in her hands and utter her spontaneous words of love and the assurance that he would later see that this was really for the best.

I cried inconsolably from the depths of my soul as the escort van backed out of our driveway with our terrified son silently pleading with his sad eyes for us not to send him away. This excruciating scene would have to serve for the rest of our lives as the last living memory of our beautiful son.

Aaron arrived in the Escalante Wilderness Area of southern Utah that same night and waited a few days for a brief intake exam, indoctrination into the rules of the program, and the issue of ill-fitting shoes and clothing. This picture of him was taken on March 8th , when he was noted as weighing 131 pounds on a lanky 5'-11" frame.

Aaron's bloody and tattered journal would contain no poetry, but would record in his own words an unbelievable account of torture, abuse and neglect; a horrific tale that is corroborated by the journals of the so- called "counselors", along with the journals and sworn testimony of his troubled young cohorts.

This calendar was assembled by criminal investigators from program records and chronicles 21 days of ruthless and relentless physical and psychological abuse and neglect. Aaron spent 14 of his 20 days on the trail without any food whatsoever, while being forced to hike 8-10 miles per day. On the days he did have food it consisted of undercooked lentils, lizards, scorpions, trail mix, and a celebrated canned peach on the 13th . On top of this, with temperatures below freezing, he endured 13 of 20 nights with only a thin wool blanket, plus 5 nights without warmth or protection of any kind. Aaron complained of severe stomach pain and asked to see a doctor as early as the third day of hiking, and by the tenth day had lost all control of his bodily functions; but unbelievably, as he got weaker and lost nearly 20% of his body weight they repeatedly refused to send him to a doctor. Taken from what appears to be the industry handbook, their policy had predetermined that these kids are all liars and manipulators and therefore "Aaron was faking."

[Slide #3] This grotesque skeleton is what Aaron looked like when he was seen the evening before he died by Georgette Costigan, the registered EMT who, still insisting that he was faking, didn't even take his vital signs, but instead took the occasion to barter a meager piece of cheese in return for his promise to try harder and hike the following day. This company employed EMT, and relative of owner Bill Henry, dismissed his final desperate plea to see a doctor who could prove he wasn't faking and made a conscious decision to prove a point rather than render aid, thus effectively killing our son rather than saving him.

What you cannot see in these photos are the bruises, cuts, lesions, rashes, blisters and open sores that covered Aaron's body from head to toe. These scars of abuse and the dried skin stretched taut over his bones are what his mother and I were left to discover without any warning when the sheet was pulled back at the mortuary. This, we screamed, could not be our son as we grabbed each other and collapsed to our knees, but the scar above his now sunken right eye told us that it was. It was in that one shocking moment of proof that our lives changed forever.

The stories of Aaron's death and the others who have died, or survived the abuses of these programs, are chilling reminders of the dangers of absolute power, and point out the extremely high risks we take in allowing these programs to operate without strict regulation and oversight.

This country, this congress and this committee are faced as never before with several urgent and critically important choices.

If we choose economic growth over human rights; if we choose no-growth-in-government over the safety of our children; and if we continue to place our faith in the self-regulation of private enterprise over the mandate of our government to protect our nation's health, safety and welfare, we are choosing to fail in our sacred obligations to our children, our families, and our future.

I implore you, as I know Aaron would, to PLEASE stop paying lip service to "family values" and start placing "value-in-families." We can do this in part, by investing the resources of the American people in our children who will soon inherit our challenging legacy; and we can START NOW by putting a stop to these fraudulent and destructive programs of institutionalized child abuse.

Respectfully,
Bob Bacon, father

In: When Abuse and Neglect Occur at Residential... ISBN: 978-1-60876-965-0
Editor: Kirsten S. Madsen pp.123-125

Chapter 10

HOUSE COMMITTEE ON EDUCATION AND LABOR*

Cynthia Clark Harvey

Thank you, Chairman Miller, and those Committee members present today for the opportunity to share our family's story. Our story is a personal tragedy, but please remember that for each family that has suffered the ultimate damage, the death of a beloved child, there are perhaps thousands of others who have suffered physical or psychological neglect and abuse. For those individual and family victims, there is no public acknowledgement of their sorrow and pain, as there has been of ours.

Our first-born, Erica, was an amazing kid—everyone says that about their own, but it's true, she was. So many times during Erica's too-short life, she'd do or say or create something that just knocked our socks off. Erica was an incredible student, straight A's, with Gifted classes in Math and Language. She was a competitive springboard diver with dozens of medals. Erica was a musician who played clarinet and drums, a prize-winning visual artist, a weekly volunteer with a local animal shelter from the time she was 10 (and dragged us along, so they got two, three or four for the price of one determined little girl.)

* This is an edited, reformatted and augmented version of a U. S. Government Committee Office publication dated October 10, 2007.

Erica's bright light seemed to flicker, when at fourteen and in the 8th grade, she began to experience mental health problems. Erica became depressed, then suicidal. She engaged in cutting behaviors. To medicate herself, she began abusing illegal drugs. Erica was hurting in many ways and our whole family was suffering.

Erica was in the care of a psychiatrist and a therapist, who both recommended that we consider a residential treatment program. Michael and I were desperate to find help for Erica. Our daughter was 15 and a half years old when we made the decision to send her to what we believed was a legitimate treatment program, a place staffed with people who could help our family move forward from some very dark times.

We compared several programs over a period of many weeks. We eventually focused in on CF because they were, and continue to be, leaders in the industry, one of the founding members of NATSAP, and of OBHIC. We chose CF because they claimed to be fully licensed, because they were JCAHO accredited, because they claimed experience with teens being treated with psychiatric medications. We, as parents, were interviewed by the program. We laid bare our hearts, our souls and our story to the program. They told us our daughter would be treated by experienced staff: experienced therapists and experienced wilderness guides and emergency medical technicians (EMTs). They touted their back country planning and emergency procedures.

They told us we could trust our most precious firstborn daughter, Erica, to them.

On May 26th, 2002, we arrived at CF's Nevada office. We had been advised by CF not to tell Erica we were placing her until our arrival for the family meeting that would begin the trek. Of all the many profound and tormenting regrets we have about our terrible decision, agreeing to deceive Erica is one of the worst. When we told her why we were there, she was shocked, angry and scared. We will be haunted as long as we live by Erica's cry of *Please, Daddy, don't make me go.*

On May 27th, 2002, the first full day of Erica's Nevada wilderness trek, CF's trusted team mistook a dire medical emergency for teenage belligerence and Erica died that afternoon of heat stroke with dehydration. Over a period of hours, Erica's condition had worsened as she was pushed to keep hiking. When Erica's eyes rolled into the back of her head and she fell off the trail, head first, into rocks and scrub brush, she was left to lie where she fell for forty five minutes, while two CF staffers, still unwilling or unable to recognize what was happening, watched Erica die a slow, painful death.

When the CF team finally responded to Erica's last few tortured breaths, they contacted their on-call medical doctor, but the "doctor" turned out not to be a doctor at all, rather a physician's assistant located in Oregon. They called the local authorities to ask for help and a helicopter to get Erica to a hospital but they didn't know where they were and sent the search and rescue team the wrong GPS coordinates. The helicopter took hours to arrive because, contrary to the advance planning that we were told to expect, no arrangements with local authorities had been made, nor was any sort of trip plan filed. Later we found out that none of the CF team had experience with administering psychotropic drugs and no training in how to evaluate those drugs' effect on an individual during a trek. We also found out that the EMT on the team was on his very first trek, had only recently completed coursework in WEMT and had never experienced a real medical emergency before.

Six days from today, October 16, is Erica's 21st birthday. The day she was born, we held her and we saw the universe in her fierce dark eyes. We filled ourselves with dreams for her. We imagined who she'd be at two, at ten, at twelve, twenty-one, thirty. Today we're left with only memories, some of them beautiful, some of them harsh, and no dreams of Erica's tomorrows.

Erica Clark Harvey October 16, 1986--May 27, 2002

In: When Abuse and Neglect Occur at Residential... ISBN: 978-1-60876-965-0
Editor: Kirsten S. Madsen pp.127-131

Chapter 11

TESTIMONY OF PAUL LEWIS, FATHER OF RYAN C. LEWIS*

Paul Lewis

Our son, Ryan lived his life to the fullest, surrounded by adoring friends and relatives. He was a Boy Scout and a fire explorer. As an avid outdoor enthusiast, he enjoyed kayaking, camping, hiking, and mountain biking. He read for hours and was a master at putting together complicated ship and airplane models. He was an all American boy with sparkling blue eyes and a big smile that lit up his freckled face and our whole world.

Ryan could weave an entertaining story and was often times hilarious in his presentation. He had a remarkable way of relating to people of all ages and could draw anyone into conversation on a variety of topics. He was sensitive to others and could articulate his views and feelings way beyond someone his age. He was a history buff and could match any adult conversation about WW1 1. In fact, one night we met two WW11 Vets in a restaurant and one remarked that Ryan knew more about the war than he did and he was there!

With all of Ryan's extraordinary qualities, he sadly suffered from clinical depression. He was a brave and courageous person who battled the darkness valiantly. But as a family, we knew that we needed help from professionals and sought help from a clinical psychologist and child psychiatrist. In addition,

* This is an edited, reformatted and augmented version of a U. S. Government Committee Office publication dated October 10, 2007.

what Ryan needed was an integrated program where he could continue his schooling and receive therapy while being among peers.

After exhausting all local resources to help Ryan, we reached out to Steve Bozak, an educational consultant. We provided him with all Ryan's educational and medical records. Given Ryan's background, he strongly recommended a Therapeutic Wilderness Program named Alldredge Academy in Davis, West Virginia. He told us this would be the safest, most appropriate place for Ryan. Ryan's psychiatrist, after speaking to the Admissions department also agreed that this might meet Ryan's needs.

Educational and medical records were then sent as well as detailed psychiatric information required on an extensive application. We were very hesitant to send Ryan so far away but the program's marketing was first rate, appearing to be just what Ryan needed. Alldredge used Ryan's love of the outdoors as a selling tool. The admissions personnel repeatedly toted their professionalism and expertise with children who had the same psychiatric diagnosis as Ryan's. On February 7, 2001 we enrolled Ryan and were again reassured by the program personnel that Ryan would be safe. We called every day to inquire about how Ryan was doing and we were assured that he was "just fine".

On February 13, only seven days into the program we were startled by a call at 11:15 at night. The news ripped through us like an explosion, tearing us into a million pieces. L. Jay Mitchell, the owner of Alldredge Academy, informed us that Ryan had hung himself. He told us that there was no indication that Ryan was in trouble, it caught them all completely by surprise and there was nothing they could have done. The next day, we flew to West Virginia and met with L. Jay Mitchell, John Weston White, and Lance Wells who repeated the same story as the night before. The story didn't make sense to me. The following day we met with the investigating West Virginia State Trooper who told us we were being lied to about the circumstances of Ryan's death.

This news was like losing Ryan all over again since, in his view, it was a death that could have been prevented. He told us was the night before Ryan died; he had slashed his left forearm four times with a program issued pocket knife. He told them, "Take this away from me before I hurt myself anymore; I can't take it anymore, I want to call my Mom and I want to go home." The counselors talked to him for a few minutes and he was told that people who could help him were coming out the next day. Then they gave the knife back to him. L. Jay Mitchell and John Weston White arrived the next day. Even though they called themselves therapists, neither of them had any credentials that would remotely qualify them as mental health professionals. In fact, L. Jay Mitchell is a lawyer. These individuals decided Ryan's desperate cry for help was manipulation so that he could get out of their program. Ryan was ignored and consequently at approximately 7:30 on a cold rainy night, desperate, alone, and abandoned, our young son hung himself.

One year later, Alldredge Academy, Ayne Institute, L. Jay Mitchell and John Weston White were indicted by the state of West Virginia for 'Child Neglect Resulting in Death'. We were adamantly opposed to the plea agreement made that allowed Alldredge Academy, the corporation, to plead no-contest in exchange for dropping charges against the individuals. Alldredge was fined $5000.00 for the horrific death of our son.

We filed a civil suit alleging wrongful death, fraud, and a tort of outrage. Once again, L Jay Mitchell was unable to defend himself and acknowledged fault. In spite of two court verdicts, L. Jay Mitchell continues in this business. In my opinion, as we sit here today, children are at great risk. Astonishingly, Alldredge continues to be a proud member of (NATSAP) National Association of Therapeutic Schools and Programs.

Losing Ryan has been devastating to our family, our friends and the people in our community. We miss him terribly and live with this nightmare every day. All we have left are our fragile memories of Ryan and wonderment of the prospects that could have been. We don't want other families to suffer the overwhelming loss of a child in this fraudulent industry. We ask you, Congressman Miller to do everything in your power to put an end to this gross abuse of our children. Thank you for this opportunity to share Ryan's story.

Our family was duped into believing that caring people would help Ryan who was struggling with a learning disability and clinical depression. We thought these were professionals who knew what they were doing. We had no idea that their interest was profit, not healing.

There are also additional details to our story that provide a deeper understanding of issues involved in this fraudulent residential facility claiming to help children by providing therapy and education. We would like to add these to the record.

For example, consider these facts: While he was in the program, Ryan was 5'1 and weighed 90 pounds. He was forced to carry a makeshift backpack with approximately 60 pounds of gear. At one point, he was restrained and had water forced down him.

In addition, Ryan was forced to hike in silence. This was critical because Ryan was very articulate and was not allowed to express his feelings. There is no therapeutic justification for such a policy.

Further, once he had cut his arm with the program-issued knife, there was no monitoring of his behavior. No buddy system was employed nor were counselors vigilant at staying with him at all times. Though he was clearly expressing suicidal thoughts and behaviors- and had been sent to the program with a diagnosis of depression--no mental health professional was consulted to determine whether he should continue in the program or be hospitalized. Nor were we even notified that he'd expressed such despair.

The program was completely unprepared to deal with cases like Ryan's. It operated under the assumption that all teenage misbehavior is "lies" and "manipulation" and that even depression is just "attention seeking," not a mental illness that warrants compassion and support. We believed we were putting our child in the care of people who knew what they were doing-- and yet the program didn't even have a protocol in place to deal with suicides. We had no way of knowing that these people had no business dealing with sick children-- there was no law in place that said they couldn't sell their services as a treatment for depression.

There were also additional signs of amateurism and complete insensitivity to the children they were supposed to be helping. For one, Ryan died at approximately 7:30 P.M. and we were not notified until 11:15 P.M., a four hour delay. Phone records show that there were 3 0-40 calls made during that four hour delay. Clearly, they were scrambling to cover up what had gone on and figure out how to make it look better.

Another example: in an early press release, Alldredge claimed that none of the other children saw Ryan. This was not true, in fact, another child found him. This child has been forever traumatized.

In violation of confidentiality rules, another early press release provided enough information about Ryan's funeral service to identify him.

Finally, in yet another press release, personnel at Alldredge claimed that all the children successfully completed the program. This was not the case. In fact, two weeks after Ryan died, another child that had been in his group, slit his wrists. He was evacuated, hospitalized, and sent home.

Four weeks into the program, a third child in his group threatened suicide in a note to his mother. He, too, went home. It was too late for Ryan.

Alldredge Academy has changed its name to Alldredge Wilderness Journey. Although he is not listed as a staff member, L. Jay Mitchell is still actively involved in the operation of the program. For parents in crisis, it would be very difficult to get an accurate history on the program.

We urge Congress to act to prevent people who do not know how to treat children with dignity-- let alone treat mental illness-- from selling their fraudulent treatment to other vulnerable parents and children. People with mental illness should have the right to safe, effective treatment that people with physical illness do-- and these predators should not be allowed to prey on them and their parents.

Prepared by Paul Lewis, parent of Ryan C. Lewis 1/30/87 – 2/13/01

In: When Abuse and Neglect Occur at Residential... ISBN: 978-1-60876-965-0
Editor: Kirsten S. Madsen pp.133-135

Chapter 12

CASES OF CHILD NEGLECT AND ABUSE AT PRIVATE RESIDENTIAL TREATMENT FACILITIES, OCTOBER 10,2007*

George Miller

WASHINGTON, D.C. – *Below are the prepared remarks of U.S. Rep. George Miller (D-CA), chairman of the House Education and Labor Committee, for a committee hearing on "Cases of Child Neglect and Abuse at Private Residential Treatment Facilities."*

Good morning.

Welcome to today's hearing on "Cases of Child Neglect and Abuse at Private Residential Treatment Facilities."

For a number of years now, I have been deeply concerned about allegations of child abuse in private residential treatment programs, which are often referred to as "boot camps," "wilderness programs," or "behavior modification facilities."

These allegations range from neglect to torture – a word that I don't use lightly.

Today, we will hear about neglect and abuse cases where the outcome was the worst one imaginable: the death of a child. We will hear testimony from

* This is an edited, reformatted and augmented version of a U. S. Government Committee Office publication dated October 10, 2007.

the parents of children who died. I thank them for joining us today and for having the courage to speak publicly about their ordeals.

It is estimated that hundreds of private residential treatment programs operate nationwide. The programs are governed by a weak patchwork of state regulations. In many states, these programs operate without regulations, licensing, or accreditation of any kind, despite the often exorbitant price of tuition.

Parents often send their children to these programs when they feel they have exhausted their alternatives. Their children may be abusing drugs or alcohol, attempting to run away or physically harm themselves, or otherwise acting out. They send their children to these programs because of the promise that staff members will be able to help children straighten their lives out.

In far too many cases, however, the very people entrusted with the safety, health, and welfare of these children are the ones who violate that trust in some of the most horrific ways imaginable.

We have heard stories where program staff members forced children to remain in seclusion for days at a time; to remain in so-called "stress" positions for hours at a time; or to undergo extreme physical exertion without sufficient food and water.

Today, we will hear even more horrifying stories, of children denied access to bathrooms and forced to defecate on themselves. Of children forced to eat dirt or their own vomit. Of children paired with older children – so-called "buddies" – whose job it is, essentially, to abuse them.

There is only one word for these behaviors: Inhuman.

This nightmare has remained an open secret for years. Sporadic news accounts of specific incidents have built a record that should never have been ignored, but shamefully was.

The federal government has completely failed to grasp the urgency of this situation.

In 2003, I urged then-Attorney General John Ashcroft to begin an immediate investigation into reports of child abuse at private residential treatment programs. The Attorney General refused, as did his successor, Alberto Gonzales.

I also wrote to then-Secretary of State Colin Powell asking him to investigate the treatment of children in facilities located overseas but serving American children and operated by U.S. companies. Secretary Powell's response was insufficient.

We will learn today that a number of these programs actually operate on federal land. Yet no federal agency – not the Bureau of Land Management, not the Department of the Interior, no one – has thought to review problems associated with these federal tenants, despite repeated incidents ending in the injury or death of a child.

No federal agency keeps official data about the number of children enrolled in private residential treatment programs, despite that fact that children are typically transported across state lines – sometimes even by force – in order to be enrolled in the programs.

This is an outrage.

In late 2005, I asked the Government Accountability Office to launch an investigation of private residential treatment programs. The GAO agreed, and I am pleased that GAO has devoted significant resources to this important issue. Today, the GAO will present case studies of programs where deaths occurred. Next year, GAO expects to release an industry-wide review, thus providing us with a comprehensive look at the industry.

In the past, it has been estimated that anywhere from 10,000 to 20,000 children have been enrolled in these programs at any one time.

I am sure that there are programs staffed by caring, professional, competent staff members, who do help to improve children's lives. Yet there are clearly a number of programs staffed by untrained, unlicensed, poorly paid staff members who simply cannot be entrusted with children's welfare. As a result, without regulations, the industry as a whole will continue to present unacceptable risks to the children it serves.

That is why, in 2005, I proposed legislation to provide resources to states to help them create licensing standards for private residential treatment programs. The legislation would also boost oversight of facilities overseas operated by U.S. companies.

This hearing, as well as the ongoing work by GAO and by the Committee's investigative staff, will help determine if that is the appropriate legislative response or if the situation demands something else.

One thing is clear, however: In light of the findings we will hear today, Congress must act, and it must act swiftly, to ensure the well-being of children participating in these programs. We can all agree that we have no mandate more urgent than keeping children safe.

I'd like to thank all of our witnesses for joining us today. We look forward to your testimony and to working with you to put a stop to these abuses.

Thank you.

http://edlabor.house.gov

In: When Abuse and Neglect Occur at Residential... ISBN: 978-1-60876-965-0
Editor: Kirsten S. Madsen pp.137-145

Chapter 13

WRITTEN TESTIMONY FOR THE UNITED STATES HOUSE COMMITTEE ON EDUCATION AND LABOR*

Jan Moss

Mr. Chairman, Mr. McKeon, members of the Committee, thank you for the opportunity to participate in this hearing. I am Jan Moss.

I am a mother of two grown children and a grandmother of three. To those of you who have spoken today of your devastating losses, I express my condolences, respect and utmost deference. I have not suffered the loss of a child. I do, however, have a nephew who suffered abuse in an offshore program.

I am here as the Executive Director of the National Association of Therapeutic Schools and Programs, generally known as NATSAP. We were established in 1999 in an effort to raise the bar of the private therapeutic programs serving children and families in crisis. Among our goals is the complete elimination of the abusive and neglectful practices we have heard about today. Clearly we still have a long way to go.

Chairman Miller, you acknowledged in your December 2005 letter to the Government Accountability Office that there are, indeed, "programs that

* This is an edited, reformatted and augmented version of a U. S. Government Committee Office publication dated October 10, 2007.

provide high-quality services to help troubled adolescents get back on track." The three personal narratives I am attaching to my written testimony underscore the value of high-quality therapeutic schools and programs. We are committed to ensuring that these programs remain available to families in dire need of help. We are working to ensure that the only programs on the market are those of the highest quality.

NATSAP is the only entity in this country working with therapeutic schools and programs to improve them. We are a trade organization. We do not provide certifications or conduct investigations.

I am attaching the Ethical Principles of the National Association of Therapeutic Schools and Programs to my written testimony. Our Principles of Best Practice are based on our 12 Ethical Principles and were formulated using the standards set by the Joint Commission, which accredits nearly 15,000 health care programs in the United States. We will not accept or retain members that do not abide by our ethics or attest to following our Principles of Good Practice.

When we receive notification of a concern about one of our members, we review evidence from state licensing authorities, attorneys general, accrediting bodies, and other third parties. If a member has acted in a manner inconsistent with the law or our Principles, we proceed on a case-bycase basis, either requiring the program to implement change, or cancelling its membership. NATSAP will review the findings of the GAO's investigation into NATSAP member programs and will take action as appropriate.

Our professional development activities include a national conference, which over 700 people attend annually. We hold six regional conferences, with an estimated total attendance of over 800 individuals. Each conference provides continuing education courses led by industry experts, university researchers, and other clinical professionals.

In 2006, NATSAP launched its first professional Journal. Dr. Michael Gass of the University of New Hampshire is the managing editor. In 2007, NATSAP launched its Research Initiative, which will provide members an affordable data-collection tool to evaluate the effectiveness of their clinical work. The University of New Hampshire will house the database, making it available not only to internal, but also external researchers. Dr. Keith Russell, University of Minnesota, has just released the results of his four years of research on outdoor behavioral treatment.

In 2007, the NATSAP Board of Directors strengthened NATSAP's membership requirements. We now require members to be licensed by the appropriate state mental health agency, or accredited by a reputable mental health accreditation organization, such as the Joint Commission.

Unfortunately, not all states have licensing requirements. We are working to address this inadequacy. We have worked successfully with the State of Utah to establish regulations for therapeutic boarding schools, which had previously escaped licensure requirements by claiming plain "boarding school" status. In Montana, we worked diligently to have appropriate licensure requirements put into place, but the stringent bill we favored lost to a less rigorous bill.

We continue to push for strong state licensure and monitoring requirements. We are hopeful that Chairman Miller, Ranking Member McKeon, and this Committee will help us in these efforts. We need your assistance.

The American Bar Association has submitted to this Committee the ABA's recommendations for legislation to assure the safety of children and youth placed in private residential treatment facilities. We are in fundamental agreement to the extent that the ABA recommends licensure and monitoring of these facilities. We expand on the ABA's recommendations by supporting licensure and monitoring of all adolescent treatment facilities, including those that are funded by public entities.

Mr. Chairman and Mr. McKeon, NATSAP extends its sincere appreciation for your commitment to eliminating deceptive, abusive, and neglectful programs by encouraging state licensure and enforcement. We are committed to working with this Committee, other organizations, and parents to draft and enact meaningful legislation to put an end to the horrific pain and suffering we have heard about today.

ATTACHMENT 1: TESTIMONY OF TREVOR MILES HEATON

Submitted to the U.S. House Committee on Education and Labor, October 10, 2007

Chairman Miller and Honorable Committee Members, I would like to thank you for the opportunity to share my testimony of hope and success with you.

To understand my viewpoint regarding the issue at hand, a brief history of my past is necessary. My name is Trevor Heaton. I am a 19 year old recovering heroin addict living in Salt Lake City. I began smoking pot at age 13. From there I rapidly progressed to pain medications and eventually became confined to a vicious heroin addiction. I have been to four different treatment facilities, both in and out of Utah. I have been admitted to the psychiatric ward several instances for drug related problems. I have also been part of the juvenile court system. I stole, lied, cheated, abused, neglected, and rationalized my way through my addiction. My story is no different than any other addict out there in such that I have the disease of addiction and must do everything in my power to keep this demon in remission.

It took years of using and several treatment programs for me to finally make the decision to change my life around. Obviously, the choice to stay sober is made by myself, and only for myself, but the treatment programs I attended were influential in helping me make this choice. The reason I did not remain sober after my first programs was do to a conscious decision on my part. The treatment centers provided me with all the necessary life skills, coping mechanisms, and tools to remain sober, but I simply chose not to apply the knowledge and skills I had been presented with. Two of the programs I went to were very impressive, and two were not. I can't blame a program for my relapses because although a program may not have been as quality as another, I was still made aware of my addiction, yet chose to ignore all the instruction I had been given.

I feel very fortunate to be alive today. I live a wonderful life and could not be happier. I am about to graduate from Salt Lake Community College with my Associates of Science Degree in Social Work. I have a 4.0 college GPA and plan to go for my Masters degree. I have a stable job. Relationships with family and friends have been restored to the fullest. I attend A.A. meetings regularly. I am on the Alumni Council of the National Association of Therapeutic Schools and Programs. I am also on the Salt Lake Mayors Coalition for Alcohol, Tobacco, and Other Drugs. As I said, life is beautiful at the moment. I have been given a second chance at life. This second chance was made possible by the many professionals and staff I encountered at various treatment centers throughout my journey. As we are all aware, the price of drug rehabilitation is quite expensive, but the lessons learned and the tools that are provided through such programs are priceless.

I am very grateful to my family for providing me with such resources as drug rehabilitation. I am also grateful for those individuals who have helped shape my life into something truly amazing. I respectfully ask that do all you can to eliminate abusive and neglectful programs while also doing whatever is necessary to preserve options for children and families in need of specialized treatment and educational services. Treatment is the greatest tool we have in the fight against addiction. I am proof that there is hope and that recovery is able to breed success and triumph. If you would like more information on my experience, you may contact me at any time. Once again, thank you for the opportunity to participate in this extraordinarily important hearing.

Respectfully submitted,

Trevor Miles Heaton
3125 West Lastrada Way Riverton, UT 84065
801-652-9540
U.S. House Committee on Education and Labor
Written Testimony of Thomas and Emily Vitale
91 East End Avenue
New York, NY 10028
917-382-9256

ATTACHMENT 2: WRITTEN TESTIMONY OF THOMAS AND EMILY VITALE

U.S. House Committee on Education and Labor

Chairman Miller and Honorable Committee Members, thank you for the opportunity to share our testimony with you. Chairman Miller, we share your urgent desire to ensure that abusive and neglectful "boot camps" and "tough love" programs do not harm adolescents in need of special care and nurturing.

However, most therapeutic schools and programs *do* provide healthy, positive environments in which children may learn while healing. Our daughter Caroline is one child who benefited greatly from a therapeutic boarding school. She had been in and out of many "regular high schools, never able to get her homework done (she is extraordinarily bright so teachers assumed she was lazy). As she spiraled into depression and self-injury, we realized she needed a school where she would be both safe and able to work on the issues that caused her to de-rail.

Caroline spent 18 months at the King George School, an emotional growth boarding school in Northern Vermont. During that time she attended academic classes, excelled in therapeutic art classes, participated in group and individual therapy sessions. At no time was she or any student there forced to participate in programs like those which you aim to eliminate. Her experience there has changed her life and ours. She is currently back at a "regular high school and is applying to college for next year. She would never have been able to do this without the support and nurturing of the King George School.

Certainly, you must eliminate abusive and neglectful programs. You must also preserve options for children and families in need of specialized treatment and educational services.

If you would like more information on our family's experience, or better yet, if you would like to hear from our daughter, Caroline, please contact us.

Attachment 3: Testimony of Alexandrine Lyons-Boyle

Committee on Education and Labor, October 10, 2007

Chairman Miller and Honorable Committee Members, I sincerely applaud your desire to ensure that abusive and neglectful "boot camps" and "tough love" programs are not able to harm children who need therapy and care, and need to get on the right track. I've seen news programs that horrified me regarding these programs.

However, I sent my daughter to a wilderness therapy program that was not a boot camp, not a tough love program, but was an outstanding therapeutic program that saved her life.

My daughter had always been a happy child, a good student, and a sweet daughter until she reached high school. At that time, for many reasons, including depression, ADD, and the innate meanness of many teenage girls (the way "her friends" treated her would make you cry), she began to abuse drugs. She was so depressed that she would lie on our kitchen floor and just cry. She went from being an A-B student in high level classes (honors and advanced grades), to receiving straight F's, and being told by the high school principal that they were processing her to have her removed from the school. She was arrested repeatedly.

When I learned of Catherine Freer Wilderness Therapy from her psychiatrist, I immediately sent her to this program. She spent 3 weeks hiking in the wilderness with 5 other teenagers, and 3 adults--two of the adults were trained counselors, and one a licensed therapist. All operated in close contact with a licensed therapist back in the home office who was in constant contact with the parents. These were wonderful, caring people, who, through their program, changed my daughters life.

They taught her self-reliance and self confidence (she had to cook for herself, set up her own tent at night, and carry her own supplies during the day). She is proud of what she did. They structured all conversation so the kids couldn't just trade war stories, but had to really think about why they had made the decisions they had made, what they wanted from life, what their values were, and were they living by those values? How had they affected the people in their lives? What was their future going to be like? For 24 hours a day, every day for 3 weeks, my daughter was in therapy--caring, educational, and successful therapy. She was also in the healing environment of nature, which is awesome and cannot be duplicated indoors.

After only 3 weeks, she was a changed person. The last day, when she walked into the room where her family was waiting, she had a huge smile on her face, she looked tanned, a bit heavier, much healthier; she looked confident and proud of herself, and happy! I was amazed! She was proud of all she'd accomplished, of how she'd changed, and she was looking so forward to sharing her experiences with her family.

Much, much more amazing is how now, six months later, she is again an "A" student, a smiling, happy person, who has excellent values. In fact, she has an appreciation for life that she never had before.

She has thanked me many times for sending her to Catherine Freer Wilderness Therapy. She changes her mind frequently now about what she will major in at college, but neither of us have any doubt that she will be a college graduate, a responsible member of society, and a good person.

I could give you much more detail, but in the interest of being brief, I will simply say that you are welcome to contact either my daughter or myself to learn more of the outstanding wilderness program she attended.

The people at Catherine Freer are very, very caring. They are NOTHING like I've seen on the news programs about the boot camps and tough love programs. *Please, please* do not lump them in with those other extremely scary, dangerous, and ineffective programs that harm children rather than helping them.

Thank you for protecting our youth from those harmful programs, and thank you for finding a way to differentiate the good from the bad in your legislation, and making sure programs like Catherine Freer continue to help children like my daughter.

Sincerely,
Alexandrine Lyons-Boyle
Mother of Leilagh Boyle
1558 Seven Pines Rd, #A2
Schaumburg, IL 60193
630-853-7183

ATTACHMENT 4: ETHICAL PRINCIPLES

The National Association of Therapeutic Schools and Programs

Members of the National Association of Therapeutic Schools and Programs (NATSAP) provide residential, therapeutic, and/or education services to children, adolescents, and young adults entrusted to them by parents and guardians. The common mission of NATSAP members is to promote the healthy growth, learning, motivation, and personal well-being of our program participants. The objective of all our therapeutic and educational programs is to provide excellent treatment for our program participants; treatment that is rooted in good-hearted concern for their well-being and growth; respect for them as human beings; and sensitivity to their individual needs and integrity.

In applying to become or continue as a member of The National Association of Therapeutic Schools and Programs, we agree to:

1. Be conscious of, and responsive to, the dignity, welfare, and worth of our program participants.
2. Honestly and accurately represent ownership, competence, experience, and scope of activities related to our program, and to not exploit potential clients' fears and vulnerabilities.
3. Respect the privacy, confidentiality, and autonomy of program participants within the context of our facilities and programs.
4. Be aware and respectful of cultural, familial, and societal backgrounds of our program participants.
5. Avoid dual or multiple relationships that may impair professional judgment, increase the risk of harm to program participants, or lead to exploitation.

6. Take reasonable steps to ensure a safe environment that addresses the emotional, spiritual, educational, and physical needs of our program participants.
7. Strive to maintain high standards of competence in our areas of expertise and to be mindful of our limitations.
8. Value continuous professional development, research, and scholarship.
9. Place primary emphasis on the welfare of our program participants in the development and implementation of our business practices.
10. Manage our finances to ensure that there are adequate resources to accomplish our mission.
11. Fully disclose to prospective candidates the nature of services, benefits, risks, and costs.
12. Provide informed, professional referrals when appropriate or if we are unable to continue service.

*As an executive of*____

a member program/program applying for membership with the National Association of Therapeutic Schools and Programs, I have signed below to indicate that our organization supports and follows the above Ethical Principles.

__________________	______________________
Signature	*Name (please print or type)*
__________________	______________________
Title	*Date*

In: When Abuse and Neglect Occur at Residential... ISBN: 978-1-60876-965-0
Editor: Kirsten S. Madsen pp.147-151

Chapter 14

HEARING ON ABUSE AND NEGLECT OF YOUTH IN PRIVATE RESIDENTIAL FACILITIES*

Allison Pinto

Thank you, Mr. Chairman and committee members, for this opportunity to testify before you today regarding the very serious problems of mistreatment, abuse and neglect of youth in residential facilities.

I am a child psychologist licensed in the states of California and Florida, an assistant professor at the University of South Florida, and a researcher at the Children's Board of Hillsborough County, a children's services council in Florida.

For the past three years I have served as the coordinator of A START: Alliance for the Safe, Therapeutic and Appropriate use of Residential Treatment. A START is a national, cross-sector alliance of mental healthcare and other child- serving professionals, as well as parents and youth, who have come together in response to growing concerns regarding the mistreatment and abuse of youth in residential facilities.

Each week, I receive phone calls and emails from concerned youth, family members and professionals who are trying to navigate the increasingly

---

* This is an edited, reformatted and augmented version of a U. S. Government Committee Office publication dated October 10, 2007.

complex world of residential services for youth, or to cope with the aftermath of their experience in residential programs. I have also spoken with a variety of individuals associated with the growing number of residential programs that are being framed as alternatives to traditional residential mental healthcare.

Many parents and professionals are shocked by the descriptions of institutional abuse that continue to emerge regarding the care that American adolescents are receiving in alternative residential programs. In disbelief, they often ask, "How do you know that these aren't just a few isolated incidents that have been sensationalized in the media?" or "How do you know that these aren't just the complaints of manipulative, "troubled teens" or disgruntled families?

In order to address these questions, and to gain a clearer understanding of the variety of residential programs now available for youth, my colleagues and I posted an online survey to systematically gather reports from individuals who participated in residential programs when they were adolescents. Within six months over 700 people responded to the survey.

The detailed descriptions that young adults have been willing to share through this survey provide data that reveal a highly disturbing phenomenon. While there are youth and families who are satisfied with the care and services they have received in residential programs, a significant number of adolescents report being mistreated and maltreated in programs across the country. To give you a sense of the nature and scope of problems that have emerged, I will be submitting for the record a preliminary summary of our survey findings, which reveal the following:

1. **Reports of mistreatment, abuse and neglect are widespread**. There were concerns relating to 85 programs located in 23 states, and in U.S.- owned programs based in foreign countries as well. More than half of the identified programs are self-described "therapeutic boarding schools," and more than one third of the identified programs are members of NATSAP.

2. **Youth are being transported to residential facilities by escort services under threat or use of force, without their consent**. Youth were transported in handcuffs and leg-irons, and experienced these practice as highly distressing – they frequently felt like they were being kidnapped with their parents' permission.

2. **Facilities are not maintaining health and safety standards**. Youth were not provided with the basics of a sanitary environment, leading to illnesses such as scabies, and staff supervision was not consistently provided to ensure the safety of program participants.

4. **Amateur psychological interventions are being conducted**. In the guise of "behavior modification," youth were required to earn their human rights to privacy, dignity, contact with family members, and peer relations – rights that are now safeguarded for all participants in licensed and regulated mental healthcare facilities. Youth were recruited and admitted on the basis of identified psychiatric disorders, but then received services that ignored established standards of care specific to their presenting problems.

5. **Educational deprivation is occurring**. In a variety of programs, youth were not receiving instruction from trained and qualified teachers, textbooks and educational materials did not meet state curriculum standards, and vacuous education is being provided in the guise of "independent study." Some students returned home to their original school settings to find themselves significantly behind and some who "graduated" from the alternative residential programs discovered afterward that the diplomas they received were not recognized by their home states or college admissions departments.

6. **Medical neglect is occurring**. Medications were administered without appropriate supervision by trained medical personnel, as well as the discontinuation of medications without physician monitoring. The absence of trained medical providers in residential programs has caused health problems to go unrecognized and untreated, in some cases leading to death.

7. **The use of seclusion and restraint is grossly inappropriate**. Seclusion or physical restraint were used as a punishment for rule violations and negative attitudes. Isolation for periods of weeks was reported, and youth described enduring painful, dangerous and humiliating restraint practices. In licensed mental healthcare facilities this would be prohibited, as seclusion and physical restraint can only be used when a person is determined to be a serious danger to self or others.

8. **Treatment is violating human rights**. Youth were deprived of food, sleep and shelter as a consequence for breaking rules or not evidencing sufficient progress in the program. Youth have been forced to endure stress positions, physical pain and fear-inducing encounters such as being taken into the woods or onto the highway blindfolded.

9. **Treatment is explicitly abusive.** There were incidents of physical and sexual abuse that youth never reported due to distrust of staff, threatening program environments, or the absence of universal access to child protection and advocacy hotlines.

10. **Youth are in distress and suffering.** Respondents expressed profound distress about their residential experiences. Comments included:

    - "It was a terrible place. Mentally scarring. I would hope NO ONE would ever have to go to a place like that. It's worse than jail."
    - "I don't ever want another child to be so abjectly hopeless or so horribly abused. I don't ever want another family to be torn up when there is the possibility of being reunited and healed."
    - "I still have bad dreams about it. I wake up shaking and nervous that I am there again. It has scarred me emotionally and I don't know if I will ever get over it."
      Some youth were informed by staff that their parents were aware of the maltreatment that they were enduring, and then felt betrayed and abandoned by their families, causing damage to their relationships that has been difficult to heal even after families have been reunited. For some respondents, the memories of their experience in alternative residential programs remain deeply disturbing and have led to a pattern of anxiety consistent with post traumatic stress disorder.

Are these reports credible? Based on the level of detail and the overall coherence of the accounts provided, and using my clinical judgment as a child psychologist, I conclude that they are very credible. If those of us who are mandated reporters of suspected child abuse were to learn of such treatment occurring in a family's home, we would be required to file suspected child abuse reports so that the concerns could be investigated. We must consider the reports of mistreatment and abuse occurring in residential facilities just as carefully.

Recognizing that the online reports provided are retrospective and are not necessarily from a representative sample of *all* individuals who attended residential programs as youth, the survey findings nonetheless provide compelling information indicating that there are far more than a few isolated cases of youth who are being mistreated and are suffering in residential programs. Because there are now hundreds of reports, related to such a diversity of programs, in such a broad range of states and countries, these reports reveal a coherent pattern of institutional maltreatment. Once a pattern becomes apparent in this manner, it is not appropriate, scientifically or ethically, to dismiss reports of maltreatment as exceptions to the norm. Rather, it becomes necessary to understand each report in the context of an evolving, societal phenomenon of institutional mistreatment and abuse, which must be acknowledged if it is to be eliminated.

Thank you for bringing attention and responding to this disturbing phenomenon, in order to safeguard and restore the well-being of American youth and families.

INDEX

A

B

C

D

M

N

O

P

Q

R

S

T

U

V

W

Y